XmAS 25th

MW00570416

Never a Dull Moment...

Walter Carter

Never a Dull Moment...

Walter Carter

Creative Publishers
St. John's, Newfoundland
1998

© 1998, Walter Carter

THE CANADA COUNCIL | LE CONSEIL DES ARTS
FOR THE ARTS | DU CANADA
SINCE 1957 | DEPUIS 1957

We acknowledge the support of The Canada Council for the Arts
for our publishing program

The publisher acknowledges the support of
the Department of Tourism, Culture and Recreation,
Government of Newfoundland and Labrador,
towards the publication of this book.

We acknowledge the financial support of the Department of
Canadian Heritage for our publishing program.

All rights reserved. No part of this work covered by the copyrights
hereon may be reproduced or used in any form or by any
means—graphic, electronic or mechanical—without the prior written
permission of the publisher. Any requests for photocopying, recording,
taping or information storage and retrieval systems of any part of this
book shall be directed in writing to the Canadian Reprography
Collective, 6 Adelaide Street East, Suite 900,
Toronto, Ontario M5C 1H6.

Cover and illustrations — Kevin Tobin

∝ Printed on acid-free paper

Published by
CREATIVE BOOK PUBLISHING
a division of 10366 Newfoundland Limited
a Robinson-Blackmore Printing & Publishing associated company
P.O. Box 8660, St. John's, Newfoundland A1B 3T7
Printed in Canada by:
ROBINSON-BLACKMORE PRINTING & PUBLISHING

Canadian Cataloguing in Publication Data

Carter, Walter C., 1929-

    Never a dull moment . . .
    ISBN 1-894294-00-9

1. Carter, Walter C., 1929-
2. Newfoundland — Politics and government — 20th century.*
3. Politicians — Newfoundland —Biography.
I. Title

FC2175.1.C37A3   1998   971.8'04'092   C98-950261-9
F1123.C37   1998

Dedicated to
my wife and best friend,
Muriel.
Our children,
Roger, Donna, David, Paul, Glenn,
Bonnie, Gregory, Susan,

and our grand children,
Dana, Geoffrey, Sarah, Krista, Melissa,
Angela, Andrew, Matthew, Jillian, Philippe,
Vanessa, Stephanie, John and Courtney.

"The family — that precious octopus from whose
tentacles we never quite escape,
nor, in our inmost hearts,
ever quite wish to."
Anon.

Contents

Welcome to Ottawa

FOREWORD

I have known Walter Carter for three dozen years.

His long career in public life justifies the first comment in this foreword being political. It is very obvious from this, Carter's first book, that he enjoyed politics and still derives a great deal of pleasure and satisfaction from that ancient profession. His "inter party movements" in each case can be traced to disagreement with his Party on matters of deeply held principle.

Walter Carter's main attributes are intense loyalty to his family, his friends and his Province. He has a genuine ability to laugh at himself. He is a "raconteur par excellence" weaving one hilarious story after another with the skill and deftness of a portrait painter wielding his brush.

Note Carter's choice of the caricature of himself by cartoonist, Kevin Tobin for this book's cover. No further proof of his ability to self deprecate and laugh at himself is needed.

So, settle down and enjoy this book by Walter Carter, a Newfoundlander who is truly "one of a kind."

Send a copy as a gift for any occasion to family members who live "Away." It will surely be appreciated.

Who should read this book? . . . the answer is simple. EVERYONE.

Ambrose H.Peddle
September 15, 1998
St. John's, NF

Out from Ship Island

The Carter family home on Ship Island in which the author was born
and raised.
Oil painting by George Carter

First Light of Day

I first saw the light of day on March 8, 1929, in the "bedroom over the kitchen" of our family home on Ship Island. Without the benefit of any kind of heat other than that provided by the wood-burning stove below, the bedroom over the kitchen was the most comfortable one in the house. A twelve-inch square grating in the floor above the kitchen stove provided some heat in the bedroom above when the stove was lit. However, since we burned wood only, it could not be banked like a coal burning stove and kept burning all night. Our fire was allowed to go out at bedtime. Then the whole house, including the one warm bedroom, cooled overnight, reaching icebox temperature before the stove was lit again in the morning.

The house would have been warming again when I arrived on the scene at nine o'clock in the morning, just as the vessel on which my father was sailing, the SS *Thetis*, was steaming past Ship Island on its way north to take part in the annual seal hunt. Ships travelling in either direction on that coast have to pass in close proximity to Greenspond, Ship Island and the other islands, including Puffin Island where a light station and a fog horn still provide a much needed service to mariners.

At a time when telephones and other means of rapid communication were non-existent, binoculars and pre-arranged signals were often used for communication between those on shore and their loved ones on the ships. And that is how my father received the news of my arrival.

It was determined that my mother would give birth around the first week in March when the sealing vessels would be heading north on their way to the hunt. It was arranged that if she gave birth to a boy, a flag would be flown on our flag pole on a point of land on Ship Island in full view of a passing ship. Two flags would be flown if it was a girl. If the ship passed by during the daytime, my father would get the message. Otherwise he would have to wait until he returned to St. John's, possibly two or three weeks later.

As the sun came up on March 8th, several sealing vessels, including the *Thetis*, were sighted crossing Bonavista Bay on a course that would take them within a couple of miles of Ship Island as they headed north. Finding it difficult to penetrate the ribbon of heavy Arctic ice packed close to land and extending several miles southward toward Cape Bonavista, they were moving at a snail's pace. By the time I was born, the *Thetis* was just south of Greenspond Island, inching its way past Ship Island through the ice. The timing of my arrival coincided perfectly with the arrival of the *Thetis*. Just as grandfather Carter hoisted the Union Jack for my father to see, it was passing Ship Island and in full view of our house and the pole on which the flag was flying. Obviously, my father received the message because a few minutes later it was acknowledged by several blasts of the ship's whistle.

I was the youngest of four children. I had one brother, Allister, and two sisters, Mary and Kathleen. A second brother would be born seventeen years later.

As far back as I can remember, ships fascinated me. Not only were they our only link with the outside world, they added a measure of colour and excitement to our coastal communities that will never be recaptured. Schooners sailing past Greenspond and Ship Island were a common sight in early summer as they headed north to fish for cod off the Labrador Coast. In the early fall we would see them again as they sailed by on their way home, most often with their decks awash and loaded to the hatches with prime salted codfish. Usually, we knew a couple of days in advance when the schooners were returning home. Their whereabouts would be relayed to the communities along the way by a passing Railway Coastal Boat or some other vessel returning from the Labrador Coast.

As boys, once we knew that the schooners were on their way home, we would spend hours on top of Greenspond Island with our spyglasses waiting for the Greenspond schooners to come around Cape Freels, the northern entrance to Bonavista Bay. Every schooner had certain characteristics that made it possible for us to tell at a glance its name, the name of its skipper and where it was from. I had no difficulty whatever identifying the *Maggie Stone*. In my eyes it was the fastest and the trimmest schooner of the lot. The moment it rounded the Cape and came in sight, I would run home as fast as my legs could carry me and break the news to my mother and to the families of the other men who sailed on her with my father and my uncle Walt.

Around the first week in March we would start our watch all over again. This time we would be watching out for the sealing vessels making their way to the hunt off the coast of northern Newfoundland. Again, we were able to identify every vessel that steamed pass our community, especially the ones on which members of our family were sailing.

Our watches marked not only the passage of ships, but also the changing seasons and years of our childhood.

Two

Growing Up On Ship Island

I have always considered myself fortunate to have been born and raised on Ship Island, Bonavista Bay. Separated by a narrow channel that forms part of Greenspond Harbour, Ship Island and Greenspond were, in the mid-1920s, connected by a drawbridge that spanned the narrowest part of the channel where previously the government had operated a small-boat ferry service.

With the construction of the drawbridge, Ship Islanders had the best of both worlds. We enjoyed the privilege of living on the most interesting and smallest inhabited island in Bonavista Bay and, at the same time, had easy access to Greenspond, one of the Bay's largest and most historic islands.

Even after the two islands were physically linked by the drawbridge, the residents of Ship Island refused to relinquish their identity as a distinct community. Ship Island was probably one of the first settled islands on the northeast coast of Newfoundland. Documents in my possession indicate that the Carter family settled on Ship Island in the early 1700s and were granted rights to substantial waterfront property on which they established a significant fishing enterprise.

Like most settlers who inhabited the coves and islands of Bonavista Bay, my ancestors on both sides of my family—the Carters and the Ponds—came out from England in the early 1700s in search of a new life. They were determined to wrest an honest living from the sea, whatever the cost. Hardy self-reliant fishermen, they carved out a way of life for themselves and their offspring, based on the Puritan virtues of hard work, independence and Christian principles.

When I was born in the family home on Ship Island in 1929, the entire western world, including Newfoundland, was teetering on the brink of the Great Depression. The hard times of the thirties, the construction boom in the 1940s with the promise of cash wages on American and Canadian military bases, and the outflow of Newfoundlanders and Labradorians to the Canadian mainland following Confederation, had a dramatic impact on Greenspond's population, and almost completely depopulated Ship Island. In the late 1950s the architects of the government's resettlement program decreed that both islands would have to go. Arrangements were made to resettle the entire population of Greenspond and Ship Island to a site on the north side of Bonavista Bay. The fact that both islands survived at all is a fitting tribute to the resilience and dogged determination of those people, including the two remaining families on Ship Island, Wilfred Carter and Sam Carter, who defied the bureaucrats and decided to stay.

The real shame of the thirties, which will forever linger in the memories of the people who lived in that decade, was the sight of so many good men, who were willing to do almost anything to make a living, having to swallow their independence and pride and resort to government relief or, as it was called, "the dole." Admittedly, there were people whose circumstances left them no choice. However, there were others who stubbornly refused to surrender and would rather have starved to death than accept it. My family were in that category.

There were times in the late thirties, at the height of the Depression, when the pantry shelves in our home were pretty bare, but my mother and father were determined to not give in.

My parents were not alone in that respect. The majority of the men and women in our community were equally proud and determined. Some were able to stick it out, others could not. One such man was a neighbour of ours. After trying every conceivable means of earning a living, he was forced to seek help from the Relieving Officer. Being a very proud person, he did not want to be seen bringing home the dole. It was bad enough having to receive it, but to be seen by your neighbours lugging it home in a brin bag was more than he could take. He thought he had a solution to the problem.

In those days, people had to haul their drinking water from the community reservoir on Greenspond Island in a barrel lashed to a catamaran. As the vehicle jolted over the bumps and ruts in the paths, it was difficult to keep the water from splashing out of the barrel. To prevent that, people would top up the barrel with snow. This is how our neighbour set out to transport his dole order from the supplier in Greenspond to his home on Ship Island. Placing the brin bags of food in the barrel on his catamaran, he covered it with snow to give the impression that he was hauling water. He rushed by our house to avoid being seen. As he passed our kitchen window, which was only a few feet from the path, his catamaran hit a snowbank and capsized, spilling the barrel and its contents on the ground for all to see. I mention this incident, not to be irreverent or to elicit a giggle, but to emphasize the extent to which proud and independent men abhorred having to take the miserly largesse of the Commission of Government.

Pride and independence were not the only virtues ingrained in outport Newfoundlanders and Labradorians in that era. There was also much ingenuity and skill. While rummaging through the ruins of an abandoned building, my brother Allister found the barrel of an old sealing gun. Obviously, it had been discarded many years earlier because it was as rusty as an old anchor. Allister, who had always wanted a gun of his own, took a shine to the gun barrel and decided to restore it. He spent several weeks carving a stock from a choice piece of juniper wood he had salvaged from the hull of an abandoned schooner that had found its final resting place on a shoal not far from Ship Island.

Working with tools that today would be considered primitive, he removed the rust from the gun barrel and patiently carved a gun stock as good as anything produced by professionals in a factory. Using a spoke-shave and the sharp edges of broken glass, he spent hours meticulously carving and polishing the gun stock until it was as shiny and smooth as the glass itself.

Once the stock was completed and the gun was ready to be assembled, my father insisted that it be put through a rigid test before Allister fired it from his shoulder. He knew from experience the consequences of firing a sealing gun that had a flaw or an obstruction in its barrel. It could burst. He once saw a fisherman lose an arm as a result of carelessly firing an overloaded muzzle-loader with a defective barrel. The other fishermen on Ship Island who, by this time, were caught up in the excitement of the impending event, shared my father's concern. Some of them had firsthand knowledge, including physical scars and missing limbs, to remind them of the hazards of a lack of respect for a loaded gun.

It was finally agreed that the muzzle-loader would be tested before it was fired in the normal way. It would be loaded with eight or ten fingers of gunpowder and shot, double the quantity normally used, and securely lashed to a fence down by the landwash, from which it would be fired. Positioning himself a safe distance from the gun, my brother would tug on the string attached to its trigger and cause it to fire.

One of the many advantages of living in a small community, especially on an island, is the sense of being part of the whole community. Events which in larger centres would pass unnoticed were of considerable importance on a small, isolated island. Consequently, when the time came to test-fire the latest addition to Ship Island's muzzle-loader arsenal, the entire community turned out to witness the event.

With the gun securely lashed to a fence, and having safely positioned himself behind a big rock, my brother tugged on the string that was attached to the gun's trigger, and off it went. For a moment, the place was like a battlefield. The smell of gunpowder, the smoke and the reverberation transformed the peaceful setting of the Ship Island landwash into what one war veteran said "reminded him of Vimy Ridge."

After the test-firing, the barrel of the muzzle loader was carefully inspected and found to be in perfect condition. However, the same could not be said of the old fishing stage that was inadvertently in its line of fire.

In positioning the muzzle-loader, my brother had unintentionally aimed it at a fishing stage perched on the rocks a few hundred feet away. Like most fishing stages, this one was propped up over the landwash on a dozen or so wooden shores and protected from the elements by rough clapboard nailed directly on the uprights.

Since indoor plumbing was a comfort not enjoyed at that time on Ship Island, the stage contained a "one-holer" on which its owner, Stanley Mullett, a retired fisherman, was comfortably seated as the muzzle-loader was being test-fired.

It seems that Stanley had just settled away on the one-holer when suddenly all hell broke loose. The stage rocked and quivered on its shores as muzzle-loader shot entered one wall and exited though the opposite, leaving a splintered, gaping hole in both walls a few inches above his head. The poor fisherman, who wanted nothing more than the opportunity to mull over a back issue of the *Family Herald* as he answered nature's call, had no idea what was happening. "And that's only half the story," he said later. "I was not about to hang around long enough to find out." Seconds after the

blast, the door of the stage swung open and through it staggered the fisherman, pulling up his trousers and trying to get his braces over his shoulders as he ran, looking for a safe place to take cover.

When it was all over, trying his best to make light of the whole affair and not appear too scared, he told some of the people who had witnessed his somewhat unceremonious retreat, "I was not sure if it was something I ate, or if the Germans had landed."

Life on Ship Island was never dull. Everything and everybody around us had value and importance: the sight of schooners in full sail as they passed Puffin Island, going to and from Labrador; the sound of a neighbour's motorboat; the fragrance of wild flowers and kelp in the springtime; the tantalizing aromas of homemade bread and fresh cod frying in a pan with pork scruncheons. Then there were the summer visitors and boat rides to uninhabited coves and islands for picnics. There was plenty of time for fun after a busy fishing season gave way to the more leisurely late autumn and winter days. It was all so delightfully simple.

While the outports differed from coast to coast and the customs varied, in many respects they were all the same. Each community had its share of characters, hang-a-shores and pranksters. My grandfather, Ethelred Carter or, as he was known, "Skipper Son Carter," was truly a character. As for how he got the nickname "Son," it seems that he was christened during the summer, while his father was fishing on the Labrador coast. Returning home in the fall, his father did not take too kindly to the name given his son and heir. Instead of calling him Ethelred, he simply called him "Son." From that time on, my grandfather was known as "Son" Carter and, in later years, as "Skipper Son Carter."

Having spent most of his life as master of his own vessel, Grandfather Carter was as familiar with the waterfront streets of Boston and other foreign ports as he was with the lanes and footpaths of Ship Island. He was approaching seventy years of age when I was born. My memories of him are limited. I wish I had known him when he was in his prime, because he was a very interesting person. He was a gentleman. I do not recall ever seeing him in public improperly or shabbily dressed. From the moment he came downstairs in the morning until he went to bed at night, he wore a dress shirt, tie and suit. Whenever he went outdoors, he wore a black coat and bowler hat, and he carried a walking cane.

I do not know how much formal education he had, but Grandfather Carter was well-versed in current affairs and could hold his own in any situation, on a stagehead with a group of fishermen, in a political meeting, or at a meeting of the Loyal Orange Lodge, of which he was a staunch, lifelong member. In recognition of his long years of service to the Orange Order, he was awarded a medal by the Sovereign Grand Lodge of Ireland. He was the second Newfoundlander to receive such a medal. The other recipient was Sir John Puddester. During my childhood days, my grandfather and I were inseparable. He took me with him as he made his daily rounds of Ship Island and Greenspond. Our first morning call would be the Post Office, to read the news bulletin posted on the board and, on mail days, to pick up the mail. We would then visit the various general stores in Greenspond, including the Union Store, owned and operated by Coaker's Fishermen's Protective Union. There, Grandfather and his friends would sit around the pot-belly stove for hours, telling stories, reminiscing and arguing, usually about politics. Grandfather Carter would rather argue and talk politics then eat, and usually he was good at the latter.

In 1935 he helped rescue and subsequently befriended a British sea captain—John Sherran—who was the sole occupant of a pleasure craft wrecked off Greenspond Island in a late summer gale. Captain Sherran spent several weeks as a guest in our home, while he arranged passage back to England. Immediately upon returning to England, in appreciation for what my grandfather and my parents had done for him, Captain Sherran gave us a long-term subscription to several prominent London newspapers and magazines, which we received regularly until the Second World War started in 1939. Over the same period we also received from the Captain scores of hardcover books of all description. At a time when access to public libraries and the news media was almost non-existent in isolated outports, the newspapers, magazines and books were treasured gifts.

As long as I can remember, I have been interested in local and international politics. I realize now that my exposure to the newspapers and other reading material sent by Captain Sherran contributed significantly to my lifelong interest in politics and world affairs. Undoubtedly, I also inherited from my father and grandfather their considerable interest in public affairs.

In those days, all Newfoundland outports had a "Grand-father Carter." Usually they were well-read, witty, articulate and leaders in their own right. In addition, there were the blood-stoppers, witches and sea-lawyers. And there were those who could put away warts, charm teeth, read tea leaves and tell fortunes. Grandfather Carter was in a class by him-self; he was an honest-to-goodness character and sea-lawyer. He was the undisputed leader of Ship Island, and was not without considerable influence on Greenspond Island. His involvement in the Loyal Orange Lodge is a matter of public record. Prominently displayed in the Orange Hall in Green-spond is the letter he wrote in 1915 to his Brother Orange-men in Bonavista North, in which he described in detail what had transpired at the Grand Lodge meeting in Belfast, which he attended on their behalf. People with problems or in need of advice visited Grandfather Carter. When Sir William Coaker came to Greenspond to organize the fishermen and establish a local of the Fisherman's Protective Union, he contacted Grandfather Carter. In fact, the Greenspond-Ship Island local of the Coaker Union was organized in our home.

In 1936 Newfoundland had a new Governor, Vice Admi-ral Sir Humphrey T. Walwyn. Shortly after his arrival in Newfoundland from the United Kingdom, Sir Humphrey began a tour of communities in a Royal Navy warship. He arrived off Greenspond Island shortly after dark and decided to heave to a couple of miles offshore and wait for morning before entering the harbour. During the evening Sir Humphrey ordered the ship's captain to put on a fireworks display for the benefit of the people of Greenspond and Ship Island, the majority of whom had never seen one.

The moment the fireworks started people became hysterical; they had no idea what was happening. The warship from which the fireworks were being fired was hidden from view by darkness and fog as it lay at anchor on the outside of Puffin Island, a couple of miles from Greenspond. The only thing visible was the rapid cascading barrage of fireworks that lit up the whole sky. It was an eerie sight. The word spread around the islands like wildfire, "The world's coming to an end! Judgement day is upon us!" People started milling around our home "to see what Skipper Son's making of it all." Most of them were already convinced that judgement day had arrived. As far as they were concerned, there was no other possible explanation for what was happening.

My grandfather went out in the backyard where people had gathered to see what was going on. Quoting the appropriate passages from the Bible to back up their theory, they frantically sought comfort from him. "What is it, Skipper Son?" they asked. "Is it the end? Are we having judgement day? What should we do? How much time do you think we have left? Where's Parson Anderson when we need him?"

Grandfather Carter remained calm, knowing precisely what was going on. Some years earlier, he had been on a vessel anchored in Boston Harbour on the Fourth of July. However, he was not about to let them off the hook that easily; not only that, he was in the mood for a bit of fun. "Maybe it is Judgement Day," he said. "Looks like it could be. In case it is, the whole damn lot of you had better get on your knees right away and ask the good Lord to overlook some of the rotten things you've done, including guzzling moonshine on the sly." In no state of mind to argue, some of them took his advice. Others tried to patch things up with their Maker as they looked heavenward from an upright position.

When Grandfather Carter was satisfied they were sufficiently humbled and had benefitted spiritually from the experience, he assured them they had nothing to worry about. "It isn't judgement day," he said.

"How do you know, Skipper Son?" they asked. "It's just like the Bible said it would be—fire and brimstone, the skies opening up, and all that. Are you sure, Skipper Son?"

"Of course I am sure," my grandfather answered. "Whoever heard of judgement day coming in the middle of the night!"

By this time, the fireworks display had run its course and, within minutes, peace and quiet had returned. Early the next morning, the warship arrived in Greenspond Harbour, and the mystery of the fire and brimstone and the skies opening up was put to rest.

As a staunch member of the Church of England, Grandfather Carter was never backward in saying what he thought of John Wesley who, as a deacon in the Church in the early 1700s, had turned his back on the Church of England and founded Methodism. It was obvious that the events of the previous evening gave him great satisfaction. "I waited a long time," he said, "to see some of these Wesleyans on their knees repenting and admitting in front of me that they aren't perfect."

Three

Uncle Walt's Catamaran

I sometimes shudder when I hear people talk about the "good old days" in rural Newfoundland, because I am reminded of the hardship and deprivation outport people suffered, particularly those who lived and raised families in the more isolated communities. While it had many advantages, growing up in places like Greenspond in the first half of this century was not as simple and carefree as the romanticists would have us believe. In many respects, life was an ongoing struggle.

Greenspond Island was first settled in the late 1600s. At that time, it had a fairly good supply of coniferous trees but, as on most small islands on Newfoundland's northeast coast, the trees were stripped away by early settlers for fuel and other uses. As a result, much of the soil was gradually eroded by the elements. The more enterprising residents were able to maintain shrubs, small vegetable gardens and patches of lawn with topsoil brought in from the nearby mainland. But since the terrain is almost devoid of vegetation and has no natural source of wood and fresh water, maintaining an adequate supply of firewood and drinking water in the days before central heating, modern-day appliances and municipal water systems was a never-ending challenge.

In those days, people who lived on Ship Island got their drinking water from a reservoir located on top of Greenspond Island. From there it was transported to their homes in buckets or, in winter, in a large barrel lashed to a catamaran. It was all downhill from the reservoir to the drawbridge connecting Ship Island to Greenspond. Consequently, it took very little effort to get a catamaran between these two points. However, it did take considerable skill, especially on Church Hill, which was quite steep and at times hazardous. As you approached the foot of the hill, the catamaran had to be carefully manoeuvred between a narrow opening between the Church of England church and the school.

Frequent use by catamarans created ruts in the snow, which acted as tracks for the vehicle as it slid down the hill, through the opening and by the church. You were safe only as long as you kept the catamaran in the tracks. With only a few inches to spare, if for some reason the catamaran left the tracks as you approached the church, you were in trouble.

On an island with no form of motorized transportation, catamarans were used extensively for hauling wood, water and just about anything that was too heavy or too bulky to lug on your shoulders. There were two classes of catamarans. One kind was used exclusively for hauling wood and bulkier objects, sometimes with a dog team. Usually, those were built sturdier and heavier, and were more difficult to handle. The other kind was smaller and daintier, and was used for hauling water, provisions and other less bulky items. This was the Cadillac of catamarans.

My Uncle Walter Carter owned one of the latter type. It was his pride and joy. An experienced master mariner, he spent most of his life on the ocean. During his lifetime, he owned and skippered several large schooners, in which he spent most of his summers fishing off the Labrador coast. The largest employer on the Island, he was well respected by the men who sailed with him, most of whom managed to eke out a better-than-average living, even in the thirties when the price of fish was at an all-time low. During World War Two, when the Labrador fishery ground to a halt, Uncle Walt was hired by the Bowater Pulp and Paper Company to pilot ocean-going vessels into Indian Bay, where pit-props destined for the United Kingdom were loaded.

Uncle Walt was meticulously neat. Everything he owned, including his seventy-five ton schooner, *Maggie Stone*, was kept in immaculate condition. It was more like a pleasure craft than a fishing vessel. He took great pride in looking after the things he had around him. His philosophy was, "If it's worth having, it's worth looking after." And that applied to everything, from his schooner to his most trivial possessions, including his catamaran. Cut by hand from a juniper log, the catamaran's two parallel wooden runners and chalks were carefully shaped, sanded and given several coats of marine enamel. Unlike the catamaran we owned, which was used to haul wood, Uncle Walt's was truly a work of art. It was light, manoeuvrable, and fast on a steep hill. When it was not in use, he stored it in his shed, where it was protected from the weather and from the young boys who frequently "borrowed" their neighbours' catamarans for a few hours of sliding on the hills.

Uncle Walt was also a very stern and austere person who did everything by the book. He was the first person on Ship Island to own a wind-charger and a battery-powered radio. The maintenance instructions that came with the batteries were quite specific: "Always use 'distilled' water in the batteries." Not your ordinary tap water, mind you, but pure distilled water extracted straight from the heavens. Aunt Emily thought it was a lot of trash. "Water is water," she would say. "It all comes from the sky." But Uncle Walt was adamant. "Who are we to question the experts?" he would say. "If the batteries call for distilled water, that is what they are going to get."

Uncle Walt was determined to follow the battery maintenance instructions to the letter. Whenever it rained or threatened to rain, he was seen by his neighbours carrying a large earthen basin, cradled securely in his arms, towards his woodshed. He would place it on the roof and leave it there overnight to catch the rain water.

At first, the neighbours didn't know what to make of it. "Why is Skipper Walt going through all that rigamarole just to catch a drop of water?" they would ask. They couldn't figure out what was wrong with the old way of catching rain water, with a wooden chute around the eave of the house and a down spout leading to a puncheon. "What's so special about catching it in an earthen basin?"

One of the more eccentric characters on Ship Island, Aunt Louie Osmond, had the answer. The first time she heard Uncle Walt's radio, she couldn't get over it. She was absolutely convinced that the voices she heard were those of little men and women inside the radio. She used to say to her neighbours, "How in the name of God is poor Skipper Walt ever going to keep enough grub on hand to feed all them little fellers in their radio? They'll eat 'em out of house and home." She was also convinced that the "stilled" water that Uncle Walt was collecting was for "them little men and women in the radio. They got to have a special kind of water, you know, not the kind we uses." I doubt that anybody on Ship Island accepted Aunt Louie's theory, but some of them were far from convinced that it was not the devil's work. "How else can you account for it?" they would say. "Human voices coming out of a box."

Uncle Walt's nightly ritual with the earthen basin intrigued the adults on Ship Island. It also aroused the curiosity of young boys who were always looking for opportunities to play pranks on their elders. As soon as the word got out that "Skipper Walt is catching special 'stilled' water in the earthen bowls to put in his radio batteries because the stuff from the reservoir is no good," the boys lost no time hatching their plan.

Before long, the water being collected in Uncle Walt's earthen bowl lost its pristine appearance and took on an amber tint. It was much like the reservoir water which, at its best, was the colour of partially steeped tea. Uncle Walt had some reservations about putting the discoloured water in his batteries, but he had no reason to question its quality. "Since it falls straight from the sky into the bowl, how can it not be pure?" he reasoned.

Uncle Walt did not know that the boys on Ship Island had seized the opportunity to have some good-natured fun. When they were sure nobody was around, they would remove the earthen bowl from the shed roof, urinate in it, and replace it. This went on for several evenings until their luck ran out. They urinated in the bowl, but it did not rain.

Removing the bowl the following morning, Uncle Walt saw that it contained about a pint of liquid. Naturally, he became suspicious. That's strange, he thought. It didn't rain a drop last night, therefore the bowl should have been empty. Where could it have come from? Not only that, it looks even darker than the other stuff I've been getting. You would almost swear it was something else. With that, he put his nose close to the bowl and sniffed its contents. Aunt Emily wondered what was keeping Uncle Walt. As she was walking towards the woodshed to see what was wrong, she heard him shouting, "Emily, come here and smell this. Our batteries are ruined. Some dirty bugger's been making his water in my bowl."

Never adverse to a good practical joke, providing it was well executed, Uncle Walt knew better than to cause a fuss or engage the Ship Island boys in open warfare. Albert and Louie Osmond had done that a couple of years earlier, and they hadn't had a minute's peace since. They were always the first to be victimized, especially on Bonfire Night when the boys would go on a rampage, collecting objects to throw on the bonfire. Uncle Walt decided to mention it to nobody, least of all to the boys or their parents. Instead, he would go out of his way to be nice to them. He would occasionally invite them to his home and encourage them to develop an interest in some of the programs, including The Adventures of Superman, a half-hour serial aired on radio on weekdays. Once they listened to a couple episodes, they would want to keep coming back to hear more. It was almost like an addiction. They would have to behave themselves or run the risk of not being invited back. There would be no more urinating in the basin. Uncle Walt's strategy worked. The water he collected in the bowl from then on was as pure and pristine as you could have it.

Uncle Walt was prepared to forgive and forget, as far as the other boys were concerned, but he was not about to do the same for me. Convinced that I was behind the distilled water incident, he was in no hurry to let me off the hook. He said, "You should have better sense than to play that kind of prank on one of the family." I remained in his bad books for several months. However, by Christmas time, things had started to improve. Uncle Walt was beginning to show signs of mellowing. When I thought he was finally ready to call a truce, I decided to put it to the test. I sheepishly asked him to lend me his catamaran to haul a barrel of water after school. He thought about it for a while. Then, to my surprise—and without even referring to the distilled water incident—he agreed to let me have it, on the condition that I have it back in the shed before dark.

I could not believe my good luck. The thrill of steering Uncle Walt's catamaran all the way down Church Hill and Post Office Lane and over the drawbridge on Ship Island was almost more than I could stand. I was not used to such luxury. Our catamaran was old and cumbersome. Its runners were so worn and rusty there were times when it had to be pushed downhill.

Hauling Uncle Walt's catamaran up the hills to the reservoir was a breeze. What a difference! I thought as I reached the top of the hill and approached the reservoir. It would take two strong men to haul our catamaran up Church Hill.

Filling the barrel with water from the reservoir was tiring and time-consuming. Using a one-gallon metal container attached to the end of a long pole, I had to dip the water through a hole in the frozen reservoir surface, then empty it into the barrel on the catamaran, one can-full at a time. Finally, when the barrel was full, I lashed it securely to the catamaran and started pushing it towards the crest of the hill. I suddenly realized that in rushing to fill the barrel, I must have spilled more water over myself than I poured into the barrel. I was drenched. As I started to descend the hill, my outer clothing was frozen as stiff as a board, making it difficult for me to move, much less manoeuvre a catamaran with a barrel of water. Before I knew it, the catamaran was out of the ruts in the hill surface and was going all over the place, completely out of control.

As the catamaran sped down the hill, water from the barrel splashed over my face. It was difficult to see where I was going. I tried unsuccessfully to regain control of the catamaran and get it back in the ruts that would take it safely through the opening at the foot of the hill and past the church. I tried digging my heels into the ice-covered surface of the hill to slow it down, but it didn't work. Like something possessed, it continued to pick up speed as it careened down the hill and headed straight for the church.

I had to make a split-second decision. Would I continue to hang on and take a chance on missing the church, or should I jump clear and let it go? I thought of being spattered against the side of the church, with the splintered remains of Uncle Walt's catamaran and a barrel of icy water splashing over me. I released my grip on the catamaran, did a few somersaults, and waited for the crashing sound as it headed directly for the church and its ultimate destruction.

Surveying the splintered remains of what was once Uncle Walt's pride and joy, and the staves of the water barrel scattered all over the ground, I knew I was in serious trouble, not only with Uncle Walt, but also with the Church of England minister and my teacher who was the church warden. The church was not unscathed either. The corner boards were torn off, and the siding was damaged in the area of the impact.

Totally dejected, I gathered up the debris, threw it in the churchyard, where it would come in handy for splits, and headed back to Ship Island. As I drew closer to Uncle Walt's home, I kept thinking, what am I going to tell him? As a sea captain, he had had his share of mishaps and near-misses, but he always said they were caused by an "act of God," never by negligence or bad judgement. Perhaps, I thought, I can use the same excuse. If I tell Uncle Walt that crashing his catamaran into the church was an act of God, it would sound much better than admitting I was negligent or showed bad judgement. Suddenly remembering the damage to the church, I decided it was not such a good idea after all. It's bad enough to have defaced God's House, I thought, but blaming it on Him would be like blaming Uncle Walt for what had happened to the catamaran. On second thought, perhaps I should simply blame the whole thing on the Devil.

After all, I figured, he's the only one who really has a motive.

Four

The Dirty Thirties: a Political Education

All things considered, my parents were reasonably well educated. Both of them went as far as they could in the school system that existed in Greenspond during that period.

Upon finishing school, my mother went to work with James Baird Limited, a large mercantile firm based in St. John's, with branches in several Newfoundland outports, including Greenspond. Like most general stores in rural communities, stores operated by the Baird company carried a wide range of merchandise, including ladies' and gents' clothing, home furnishings and provisions. In addition to her other duties, my mother was also the buyer for the Greenspond store. In the spring and fall, she would visit the company's St. John's store and select clothing and other merchandise for the Greenspond store for the coming season. At a time when jobs were at a premium, especially for women, my mother was better off than most of her contemporaries.

After my father finished school, he studied wireless telegraphy. His training complete, he went to work with the Newfoundland Department of Post and Telegraphs and was assigned the position of Post Master in Salvage, Bonavista South. However, sitting at a desk ten or twelve hours a day, sorting mail and receiving and transmitting telegraph messages in Morse code, was much too structured and confining for my father. Less than a year after receiving the appointment, he resigned and returned to Greenspond, where he spent his next 20 years enjoying the freedom of fishing off

Labrador in the summer and early fall with his brother on their 75-ton schooner, *Maggie Stone*, and going to the seal hunt in the spring with his old friend, Captain John Dominey, on the SS *Neptune*.

All my forebears, on both my mother's and father's side, followed the same pattern. They sailed their small schooners up the Labrador coast, and followed the cod wherever it and the winds and tides took them. In the spring they were off to the seal hunt. The rest of the time they cut pulp wood, worked on construction jobs, or at whatever came along.

In the mid-thirties, my father was elected local chairman of the Fishermen's Protective Union. It was headed by Kenneth M. Brown, who in 1936 succeeded William (later, Sir William) F. Coaker as President. Brown had a colourful and checkered political career. He was one of my earliest political idols. (People who have observed my political career will, I am sure, draw certain conclusions from that statement.)

In 1923 Brown was elected in Twillingate District as a Liberal under Sir Richard Squires. He was re-elected as a Liberal under Albert E. Hickman in 1924, and again under Squires in the 1928 election. In 1932 he joined the Alderdice Tories and was elected as the member for Grand Falls District and subsequently appointed to the Alderdice cabinet. In 1946 he successfully contested Bonavista South District and became a member of the National Convention.

I first met Ken Brown late in the fall of 1938, in St. John's in the lobby of the Newfoundland Hotel, where he and the local chairmen of the Fisherman's Protective Union were attending an executive meeting. When I learned that my father was going to St. John's to attend the meeting, I persuaded him to take me with him; I wanted to meet Ken Brown. I was nine years old at the time.

The trip turned out to be an adventure in many ways. The ocean on Newfoundland's northeast coast is seldom smooth but it is never smooth in November. We boarded the Newfoundland Railway coastal boat, the SS *Home*, in Greenspond en route to St. John's. From the time we left until we entered St. John's harbour three days later, it blew a living gale.

Growing up on an island in Bonavista Bay, without electricity, cold storage facilities or other such amenities, we weren't used to much variety in our diet. Foods that required refrigeration, such as fresh meat, poultry and dairy products, were out of the question. However, there was never a shortage of fish and wild game, including ducks, turrs and rabbits, all of which were available as needed without having to be frozen and kept on hand for long periods of time. The sleeping accommodations on the *Home* left something to be desired, but the same could not be said of the meals. The quality and variety of the food served on the Railway coastal boats in those days included frozen desserts, fresh fruit and other fare unheard of in most outport homes. I was not about to let a northeast storm or anything else interfere with my appetite, even if I had to crawl to the galley on my hands and knees.

While most of the other passengers were in their berths, moaning and groaning from seasickness and unable to stand the sight or smell of food, I didn't miss a meal. Nor did I miss a chance to have seconds and generous servings of dessert. My father knew the captain of the *Home* and we frequently ate at his table, which was a special treat.

There were several other treats in store for me on that trip. One of our ports of call was Port Union, Trinity Bay. As we approached the wharf, I could hardly believe my eyes. A monstrous animal, harnessed to a cart loaded with barrels, was standing still on the wharf. I had seen pictures of horses, but since there were no such animals on Greenspond Island or Ship Island, that was the first one I saw in the flesh. I couldn't dream they were so big. How can such a huge animal be so tame? I thought. Even the crackies in Greenspond aren't that tame.

The next treat in store for me came when we docked in St. John's and I had my first ride in an automobile. What a great way to travel! I thought as we headed down Water Street to visit one of my father's old friends on Bannerman Street.

And that is where I had my first introduction to an indoor flush toilet. The toilet was located in a small, unfinished basement room, with barely enough headroom for a person of average height to stand upright. Hanging from the ceiling, directly above the toilet, was a pull-chain electric light socket and bulb. Seated, I marvelled at the comfort compared to the outdoor, one-hole variety that we were used to on Ship Island. There was only one problem—when I closed the toilet door it was pitch black; the electric light hanging from the ceiling would not come on. I pulled the chain several times and nothing happened. I decided to remove the light bulb and check the socket. Still comfortably seated, I held the socket in one hand and with the other started to explore the inside of the socket. As my fingers came in contact with the metal, I literally got the shock of my life. I'm unable to find adequate words to describe the psychological impact—not to mention the immediate physiological impact of the electrical shock. Suffice it to say, it left me with a lifelong terrible fear of electricity.

Later that day, I was in for the biggest treat of all. I met my idol, Kenneth M. Brown. Towering above the people around him in the hotel lobby, he greeted the local chairmen as they arrived for the meeting. Spying my father, he came over and shook his hand. Looking down on me, he boomed, "And who is the young man with you, Brother Carter? Is he your vice chairman?" What struck me most about Brown was his huge physical stature. I shall never forget how excited I was when we shook hands. I would have some story to tell my school chums when I returned to Greenspond, "I met Kenneth M. Brown and actually shook his hand!" And not only

that, I was allowed to sit in on the executive meeting with Brown and the union chairmen.

My father's politics had an ally in his flair for writing. As a regular contributor to the editorial pages of the *Fishermen Worker's Tribune*, the official publication of the Fishermen's Protective Union, he availed himself of every opportunity to vent his anger and contempt for the Water Street fish merchants and their "soul mates" as he called them—the Commission of Government. This non-elected, British-appointed body had ruled the country since Newfoundland relinquished self-government in 1934.

Both my father and my grandfather Carter stubbornly refused to acknowledge the Commission of Government's right to govern Newfoundland. They viewed the Commissioners as a bunch of dictators who were totally insensitive to the needs of the outports, and too close to the Water Street merchants, most of whom amassed fortunes on the backs of the fishermen. While they were paying fishermen a mere fraction of the true value of their fish and, in some cases, cheating on the fish culling and weighing methods, Water Street fish merchants lived like emperors in their spacious, palatial mansions, surrounded by all the trappings of power and wealth. Evidence of their ill-gotten wealth can still be seen in certain St. John's neighbourhoods, where imported wrought-iron fences and stately homes serve as vivid reminders of their greed. Evidence can also be seen in some of their offspring who desperately cling to the remnants of their families' one-time dominance of the social, political and economic life of the province. My father's hostility towards the Commission of Government was not without cause.

There were other reasons, too, why Father had no love for the Commission of Government. Shortly after he became local chairman of the Fisherman's Protective Union, the Commission of Government sent Whitfield Laite, a field worker with the Department of Natural Resources, to Greenspond on a special assignment. He was to recruit fishermen to move with their families to the Eastport Peninsula, where they were promised generous government assistance to help clear and cultivate farmland. It was part of a co-operative land resettlement program initiated by the Commission of Government to encourage fishermen to farm as a means of diversifying the Newfoundland economy and reducing their dependency on the fishery.

On the surface it looked like a good deal. However, the fishermen who were talked into going quickly discovered that the transition from fisherman to farmer was not as simple as the government's agent would have them believe. They also discovered that it always pays to read the fine print in any legally binding agreement before you sign it. It seems that Laite did a poor job of explaining some of the details. Obviously, he was instructed by his superiors in St. John's to use every means at his disposal to produce results. In fact, it was alleged by those who signed up that he deliberately misled them. Nevertheless, fifteen or twenty desperate families accepted the government's offer and headed to the Eastport Peninsula where they hoped to start a new life away from the drudgery and uncertainty of the fisheries.

Things did not work out as planned. Sticking it out for a couple of months, the men decided among themselves that farming was not for them. If they were going to starve to death, they might as well be in Greenspond doing the thing they liked best: being on the water, fishing. Without further ado, they gathered up their few belongings and headed back to their homes in Greenspond, where they found out that Laite had failed to mention another important detail before they signed on. It was written in the agreement that if they refused to stay for a certain period of time and work the land as agreed, they would forfeit their right to any kind of government relief. The upshot of that action had grave consequences for the families concerned. With nothing in their homes to eat and no means of obtaining anything, they were literally facing starvation. They looked to my father, the local chairman of their union, for help and leadership.

Early one morning, while most of the people on Ship Island were sleeping, twenty or more hungry and desperate men, with nowhere else to turn, walked across the drawbridge connecting Greenspond to Ship Island and, in single file, came up the narrow footpath leading to our house. My father, seeing them coming, waited in the doorway and invited them into the kitchen, where he and my mother gave them something to eat. As they were eating, they took turns telling stories of the hardships they had experienced and the hope-lessness of the situation they had encountered when they arrived on the Eastport Peninsula. I sat back and listened attentively to what the men were saying. I could hardly believe what I was hearing. My father is right, I thought. Them shaggin' Commissioners should be tarred and feath-ered and sent back to England where they came from.

As soon as the telegraph office opened, my father sent an urgent telegram to Sir John C. Puddester, the Commissioner for Public Health and Welfare, explaining the seriousness of the situation and demanding that assistance be made avail-able without further delay to the families concerned. He also wired FPU President Ken Brown a similar message. Within a couple of hours, a telegram from Brown arrived, advising my father that the problem had been resolved and that he should personally accompany the men to the Relieving Office in Greenspond to make sure that relief orders were issued. Even though I was only eight years old at the time, the memory of that incident and the sight of those hungry, desperate men stayed with me for a long time. It also instilled in me an instinctive dislike for the Commission of Government.

Five

The Paying Guest

At the height of the Depression in the late 1930s, when money was scarce and fish prices were at an all-time low, my mother determined to wage her own war on hard times. She decided to open a boarding house and cash in on the business generated by commercial travellers who visited Greenspond on a regular basis, soliciting business from the local store owners for the wholesale houses they represented in St. John's.

Built by my grandfather in the late 1800s, our family home on Ship Island was roomy and considered at the time to be quite substantial. While it lacked practically all the amenities that are taken for granted today, such as running water, central heating and electricity, it was very well constructed and located on a point of land that was exposed on three sides to the Atlantic Ocean.

After sprucing up the spare bedroom, my mother let the word get around that our home was open for boarders and lodgers or, as they are more fashionably known today, the bed-and-breakfast clientele.

Before the advent of the telephone and other means of rapid communication, most of the wholesale houses in St. John's had salesmen or, as they were called, "commercial travellers." They travelled around the Island several times a year with huge hampers containing samples of their merchandise. Usually, they arrived on the railway coastal boats and set up a temporary showroom in the community hall where, for three or four days, they displayed their wares for the benefit of the local merchants who ordered what they needed to replenish their stocks.

Commercial travellers were looked upon by the local residents as big shots. They were well dressed, smoked tailor-made cigarettes as opposed to the roll-your-own Target and Bugler tobacco smoked by the locals, and as a rule they were generous.

At a time when most outport Newfoundlanders hardly knew what a dollar bill looked like, the St. John's commercial travellers were an impressive lot. The arrival of any stranger in the community in those days would cause a stir, but commercial travellers were different. They were welcomed by everybody, including the store owners who were anxious for new merchandise and the news from St. John's. They were especially welcomed by boarding house owners who depended on their business for a "bit of cash," and by the young boys in the community who stood to make a half dollar moving their hampers to and from the wharf and the community hall.

The going rate for board and lodging in those days was fifty cents a day. For that, you would get three hearty meals, a snack before going to bed, and a feather mattress piled high with multi-coloured, handmade quilts.

Our first customer was Rodney Pike, a regular visitor to Greenspond who travelled for one of the St. John's wholesale firms. Short, stocky and well-groomed, Pike was undoubtedly the most popular commercial traveller of the lot. He never failed to patronize social events like the soup suppers put off by various groups, including the ladies of the Church of England Women's Association who were noted for the quality of their soup and hot-cross buns. Pike was never mean when the time came to pay for his soup. He made it a point of giving a generous tip, which was a rarity in those days. He would also treat the children to a five-cent, homemade ice cream cone.

I am not sure which strings my parents pulled to get Pike's business, but having him board at our home not only meant a "bit of cash" for the family but, as the economists say, it had a "significant multiplier effect." It gave me an opportunity to run errands for him after school and almost guaranteed me the job of moving to and from the wharf on my wheelbarrow the large hampers in which he carried his samples.

Initially, Pike intended to be in Greenspond for three days. The coastal boat service operated by the Newfoundland Railway provided a weekly passenger, mail and freight service to Greenspond and other northern communities from early spring until the bays froze over in late fall. The vessel on the St. John's to Lewisporte run would call in at Greenspond and other communities on its way north. It would then turn around and head back to St. John's, calling at the same communities again to pick up passengers, mail and freight bound for points south to St. John's. Under normal conditions, a return trip took three days unless, as was often the case at that time of year, Mother Nature intervened.

On the third day, as Pike was getting ready to leave, a northeast gale came up, making it impossible for the coastal boat to enter Greenspond Harbour. The only other means of getting to St. John's in those days was a six-hour voyage in a small passenger boat to Gambo, where you would board the east-bound train on Sunday evening, terminating your trip in St. John's twelve or fifteen hours later.

The northeast coast of Newfoundland is noted for its bad weather, especially in late fall when gale-force winds and driving snow often disrupt shipping and all other marine-related activity for days. It is also noted for navigational hazards and the mishaps that have occurred there regularly as a result. The prevailing winds in the fall are generally from the northeast, and they sometimes blow relentlessly for several days at a time.

Scarcely a year passed when there was no shipwreck off Greenspond Island, and scarcely an autumn went by that the northeasterly gales failed to assert their titanic force. Salvaging cargo, and sometimes the ship itself, was regarded as a cottage industry in Greenspond during the Depression years. In fact, there were people in St. John's who were convinced that "Pond Island wreckers" aided and abetted Mother Nature through questionable means to cause vessels to run aground.

There is an old adage, "It's an ill wind that does not blow somebody good." It is fair to say that those of us who stood to profit from Rodney Pike's extended stay in Greenspond had mixed feelings about that particular storm. I dread to think how confused the good Lord must have been during that period. I have a feeling that instead of the things that seafaring families like ours usually prayed for, the prayers being offered from our home during Rodney Pike's visit were most certainly not for calm seas and fine weather. We did, however, try to make Rodney Pike comfortable.

The only source of heat in our home was an Ideal Cook wood-burning stove in the kitchen which, for safety reasons, was never kept burning after bedtime. There was a small parlour stove in the front room but, as in most outport homes, it was more of an ornament than anything else. Usually, it was coated with a silver-coloured stove enamel and was lit only on very special occasions.

The most comfortable bedroom in our home during the late fall and winter months was the one directly over the kitchen. It had a grating in the floor over the kitchen stove which provided a minimal source of heat. Normally, my mother and father slept in that room, except on special occasions. If there was someone special visiting, or if one of the children was ill and confined to bed, my parents would move to another room and let the others sleep in the "heated" room. Mother and Father gave up this room to

NEVER A DULL MOMENT...   Out from Ship Island

accommodate Rodney Pike. After all, he was our first paying guest and deserved the best we had to offer. Not only that, we wanted to make the right impression so he would come back.

Even though my mother seemed distraught over "poor Mr. Pike's misfortune," I was not convinced that her prayers differed from those offered by the rest of the family. After all, when the Water Street fish merchants were paying fishermen less than two cents a pound ($1.80 a quintal) for top quality, sun-dried salted fish, fifty cents a day was not to be sneezed at.

People who live on small islands are noted for being a different breed of people. Being isolated for long periods of time because of bad weather, being surrounded by heavy Arctic ice, being cut off from the outside world for four or five months of the year—-this was of no great concern. You learned to live with it. After a while, however, isolation became disruptive and monotonous. Food supplies ran short, and travel to and from the island was impossible, except for the more adventurous ones who walked—and sometimes crawled—over the bay ice to reach their destination. The weather played a dominant role in our everyday lives on the islands, which is why everybody engaged in weather-watching.

One of the more scientific forecasting methods was the barometer, or "weather glass." Most fishermen had weather glasses in their homes and could predict the weather with incredible accuracy. With a gentle tap on the weather glass's face, they could tell when a storm was going to hit, its severity, when it was at its height, and when it would start to abate. When the hand on the weather glass was going down, you could be sure the worst was yet to come. The moment the weather-glass hand stopped, you knew the storm was at its height; when it started to go up, you knew the worst of the storm was over and fine weather was in store.

Even though I wished no misfortune on Mr. Pike, I must confess that I did take an unusual interest in the weather during the week he was stranded in Greenspond. I tapped the weather glass three or four times a day and paid close attention to the usual signs, such as cloud formations and animal behaviour—-especially that of roosters, whose prolonged and vigorous early morning crowing was a sure sign of approaching bad weather. I also took a special interest in the older people who had chronic back problems, particularly those with rheumatism. It was a well-accepted fact that the older folks could predict the weather by the stiffness in their joints and other aches and pains associated with old age. It has been said that rheumatism was Mother Nature's first primitive effort to establish a weather bureau. A sudden increase in sales of Minard's Liniment or Radway's Ready Relief was another sign that we were in for a spurt of bad weather.

All during that week, I would be out of bed at the crack of dawn to check on the wind direction and look for other signs of weather change. If there were no such signs, I would lose no time breaking the news, first to my mother and father and then, in a somewhat more sympathetic, sombre tone of voice, to our star boarder, Rodney Pike. My mother always managed to give the impression that she was distraught. "I don't know what poor Mr. Pike is going to do, I hope that his employers in St. John's will understand," she would say, trying hard not to appear pleased. "I suppose if it's the Lord's will, there's not much anybody can do about it."

All week, a northeast gale, with high seas and wet snow, lashed Greenspond Island, bringing everything to a standstill. At the outset, being stormbound in Greenspond appeared not to cause Pike too much concern. He seemed to be enjoying it. November was usually when the churches and lodges had their social functions, or "times." Soup suppers were by far the most popular fare, and undoubtedly the most profitable one. Almost every night during his stay, there was a soup supper in one of the halls, and Rodney Pike missed none of them. However, as the storm dragged on, Pike showed signs of restlessness and obviously had had his fill of soup. He confided to me that he didn't want to see another bowl of rabbit or turr soup if he lived to be a hundred.

On the fourth day of the storm, I got up as usual at the crack of dawn to check the weather signs. Seeing no change in the wind direction—it was still blowing a gale from the northeast—I turned my attention to the animals. Perhaps it was wishful thinking, but I sensed that they were more restless and agitated than usual, which I interpreted as an indication that the storm was far from over.

One of the most reliable harbingers of bad weather on Ship Island was Peter, Aunt Carrie Carter's rooster. Named after her late husband, Peter was Aunt Carrie's pride and joy. It was a most unusual bird. With its crested head and brilliant, multi-coloured feathers, it strutted around more like a peacock that an ordinary barnyard rooster. It actually gave the impression of being arrogant or, pardon the pun, cocky. Its demeanour did not go unnoticed by the local residents, especially the younger ones who seemed to take a perverted pleasure in playing practical jokes on Peter.

Like the time he arrived home in the early morning with his legs tied. Aunt Carrie was out in the yard feeding the hens when she saw Peter staggering down the lane as if he had been on an all-night drinking binge. He would make a few short steps and roll over on his side. He would return to an upright position, make another couple of steps, and roll over again. It seems somebody had tied Peter's legs, leaving only enough slack to enable him to make very short steps. It probably took him all night to get home.

Then there was the morning Peter mysteriously turned up, perched on a small bowl-shaped rock about a foot in diameter and a hundred feet offshore in the middle of Ship Island Harbour. Because of its shape and size, the rock was referred to by local residents as the Chamber Pot. At low tide

the Chamber Pot protrudes above the harbour surface, but at high tide it all but disappears. Obviously, the tide was low when Peter sought refuge on the Chamber Pot. However, as the tide came in, it slowly disappeared beneath the surface, making it appear that Peter was standing on the water. That was the sight that greeted Aunt Carrie and the rest of the people of Ship Island that morning.

Naturally, speculation was rampant that day on Ship Island as to how Peter had managed to get himself into such a predicament. After all, roosters are not noted for being great swimmers. The more superstitious people were convinced that it was the work of an evil spirit or supernatural power. I knew what had happened. However, since Peter was not injured, and I was already a prime suspect in the leg-tying incident, I decided to say nothing. Not only that, I was having too much fun listening to the others as they conjured up all sorts of weird and wonderful stories about Peter's latest escapade.

Here is what happened. I arrived home around eleven o'clock the previous night with a week-old chick I won in a card game. I decided to take it directly to the hen house, which was perched on the edge of a bank overlooking the harbour, and put it in with the other hens. As I opened the hen house door, Peter, who was paying a social call, came flying out and, in the darkness, lurched over the bank. I had no idea where Peter went, and because it was pitch dark, I had no way of finding out. The tide was low so I took it for granted that he was safely perched on the landwash below. Obviously, I was wrong. It seems that Peter had landed in the water and floundered about until he found refuge upon the Chamber Pot.

Peter's narrow escape did nothing to impair his image or his credibility as a forecaster of foul weather. Whenever a storm was approaching, Peter would swagger down the narrow path, usually followed by his harem of admiring fowls, and head directly to a ledge overlooking the harbour, where he would flap his wings for a few seconds, then crow. Peter was quite a performer. Like the town criers of old, the more unsettling the message, the louder he crowed. That morning he was at his best. As if he sensed what was going on, Peter seemed to get a perverse pleasure out of being the purveyor of yet another unfavourable weather forecast.

I had observed all the usual signs, and it was obvious that Rodney Pike would be spending another day in Greenspond. I could hardly believe our good luck. Another day, another half dollar, I thought, as I hurried into the kitchen and up the stairs to my mother's bedroom to break the news. I was so excited, I could hardly wait to see the look on her face. I was still not convinced that her outward expression of grief over "poor Mr. Pike's predicament" was as sincere as she would have us believe. I wasted no time knocking on the door of her bedroom. I barged in and blurted out, "We got Pike for another day, Mom. It's still blowing a living gale outside!"

In the excitement, I completely forgot that Rodney Pike was occupying the room my parents normally slept in. There was Pike, lying on the bed and wide awake, snuggled under the blankets, with only the upper part of his face visible.

I tried to make light of what had happened. But Rodney Pike needed no explanation. Having spent most of his adult life travelling around Newfoundland and living in boarding houses, he knew the economics of maintaining a boarding house—an empty bed generated no revenue. He also knew that boarding house operators were never anxious to get rid of paying guests, even if it meant running the risk of appearing to conspire with Mother Nature.

There is an old Danish proverb, "Fish and house guests stink after three days, but a paying house guest is a horse of a different colour." And Rodney Pike was a paying guest.

Six

Wedding Bells and Flying Caplin

If you have never walked or stumbled through lines of men armed with six-foot muzzle-loaders being fired off simultaneously, it is safe to say that you never attended a Newfoundland outport wedding, took part in a political rally, or witnessed an Orangeman's New Year's Day parade on the northeast coast of Newfoundland.

Holidays, athletic contests, religious observances, and other festivities are celebrated the world over with parades and pageants. Athletic and historical events provide the occasion for most of the parades and pageantry in the United States. In Roman Catholic countries, there are Holy Week processions in many towns and cities. One of the best-known annual celebrations with religious roots is the Mardi Gras in New Orleans where Shrove Tuesday, the last day before Lent, is celebrated with carnivals, masquerade balls, and parades of costumed merrymakers. In England the coronation of a monarch, royal weddings and other historic events are highlighted with fireworks and, frequently, the reverberating bursts of cannon fire and musketry.

When I was a young lad growing up on Ship Island, guns were an essential part of outport life—every fisherman owned one. In fact, some had an arsenal of guns, including muzzle-loaders, breech loaders, and rifles of all descriptions. Not only were guns used for hunting seals and other animals for food, they were also the Newfoundlander's traditional way of expressing affection and celebrating such special events as weddings, parades and political rallies. It was their way of applauding the participants and showing approval. There were other special events including the Orangemen's Parades on New Year's Day that called for great celebration.

On my family's fishing room on Ship Island lay an old abandoned cannon, slowly sinking into the ground. Crafted out of cast iron, it was about six feet in length and must have weighed more than three hundred pounds. It was one step removed from the catapults, slingshots and other primitive weapons used by military leaders, before the appearance of gunpowder in the 13th century, to hurl large stones, spears and arrows at their enemies. It was crude and clumsy, its only embellishment being a half-inch hole at the end of the muzzle, into which the fuse was inserted and the gunpowder charge ignited.

There is nothing on record to indicate how the cannon got in my family's possession. The most likely story is that it was left there by the French in the early 1700s, when the Treaty of Utrecht gave the French certain rights to the coastline extending northward from Cape Bonavista, which included Greenspond.

In 1939 a Greenspond family was busily making plans for the upcoming marriage of a daughter who was about to "make a good match." The groom-to-be was a promising young Church of England minister who had just arrived in Greenspond from Oxford University, where he had graduated with a degree in theology and was subsequently ordained.

My father felt that such an event called for a special celebration. After all, not every day does an ordained Church of England clergyman become a member of a Greenspond family. Of course, he thought, there will be a battery of muzzle-loaders and the usual homemade firecrackers ready for the occasion, but surely the wedding of an ordained clergyman, especially to a local young woman, calls for something special. Perhaps he thought he could re-activate the old cannon and give the bride and groom a real sendoff. Securing the quantity of gunpowder needed to load the cannon and do justice to the occasion would be no problem; he still had a full keg left over from the previous year's seal hunt. He knew it would have to be kept secret, not only from the bride and groom, but from the whole community, for it to have the desired effect.

A week or so before the wedding, my father spent most of his spare time preparing the old cannon for the big event. He tried to be as inconspicuous as possible as he removed the caked-on rust, and positioned the cannon at the right angle to get the maximum effect when it was fired.

Our neighbours on Ship Island were completely baffled. Since the cannon had been lying there unnoticed for generations, they failed to understand why my father was suddenly taking such interest in it and propping it up as if he were preparing to fire it off. We were one of the first families on Ship Island to own a radio and have access to world news—perhaps they feared that my father knew something they didn't about the situation in Germany, where a lunatic by the name of Hitler was starting to act up.

For days they were in a quandary. "What in the name of God is he up to?" they asked each other as they watched my father restoring the cannon and struggling singlehandedly to prop it up. Never averse to causing a bit of mischief, my father did nothing to squelch their suspicions. In fact, he deliberately kept fuelling their curiosity by dropping hints that he was sprucing up the cannon "in case something happens."

With their curiosity getting the better of them, and becoming more convinced by the day that my father knew more than he was telling them, our neighbours' visits became more frequent. They would drop by several times a day to hear the news. "What's happening on the other side?" they would ask. "Is that fool Hitler still bawling and shouting?" Despite the lack of communication with the outside world, it was common knowledge that the world was on the brink of war.

There was one wily old character who lived a few hundred feet down the lane from us on Ship Island, who had a very good idea what my father was up to. For years, Bobby Carter and my father were noted for playing pranks, sometimes on each other. Bobby was still waiting to pay my father back for a prank he had played on him the previous New Year's Day.

Following a long-established tradition, on New Year's day members of the Greenspond Orange Lodge and the Orange Young Britons engaged in a daylong celebration. Preceded by their brass band and with Union Jacks fluttering from every flag pole, they paraded in full regalia around Greenspond and Ship Island to the tune of "Onward Christian Soldiers," or another spirited Protestant hymn. It was customary for them to conclude that part of their celebrations by attending a church service. After lunch they would assemble in the Orange Hall, where the men would dole out handfuls of common candies and peppermint knobs to the children, while the women were busy peeling vegetables and preparing for the evening meal. In the evening they would re-assemble in the Orange Hall for a hot supper, usually salt beef and cabbage, a square dance, and a "drop of homebrew."

That year, as the Orangemen paraded in single file along the narrow footpaths on Ship Island, they were horrified to see King William of Orange being hanged in effigy from the top of "Brother" Bobby Carter's flagpole. As if that were not bad enough, it was hanging above the Union Jack, which was flying upside down. To hang anything above the Union Jack is sacrilege, but to hang the Union Jack upside down—well, that's high treason.

Like his father before him, Bobby Carter was a staunch Orangeman. As he had done for years, Bobby left home early that morning to help organize the parade on the grounds near the Orange Hall. While he was gone, my father got an old suit of combination fleece-lined underwear, stuffed it with straw and, a few minutes before the parade arrived, draped it with Orange Lodge regalia and hoisted it on Bobby's flagpole.

Even though Bobby had to take some good-natured ribbing from his fellow Orangemen, in the parade, he took it in stride and tried to laugh it off with the others. He instinctively knew, however, that my father was the culprit. He also knew it would only be a matter of time before he got even.

He did not have long to wait. Bobby Carter knew that my father's sudden interest in restoring the old cannon was for a reason. He was up to something, and Bobby had a pretty good idea what it was: the upcoming wedding of the new rector. Using his spyglasses, Bobby watched my father's every move on the day of the wedding. He spied him as he tried to make his way along the landwash, carrying a suspicious looking container and heading towards the cannon. Still looking through his spyglasses, Bobby watched my father carefully pour the contents of the container down the barrel of the cannon, ram it down with a wad of oakum, and make a few last-minute adjustments to its position, obviously in preparation for the firing. It did not take Bobby long to put his own plan into action.

Satisfied that everything was ready to go, and that his plan was a well-kept secret, an hour before the wedding ceremony was to commence my father left the cannon unattended and went home to get dressed for the reception that would follow the church ceremony. That is when Bobby Carter executed his plan.

With a four-gallon bucket of soggy caplin, Bobby sneaked around the shoreline to where the cannon was located and rammed the caplin down its barrel. He then placed a wad of oakum in the cannon's barrel and tamped it down.

Earlier that afternoon (realizing that he needed an ally to help him execute his plan) my father had pulled me aside and told me what he planned to do. He said he wanted me to stand near the church entrance during the ceremony and, at the appropriate time, give him a signal to light the fuse. He wanted to fire the cannon the moment the bridal party emerged through the church doors. Timing would be very important. I would have to let him know, using a prearranged signal, the moment the ceremony ended and the bride and groom started walking towards the church door. He would need a few seconds lead-time to light the fuse and wait for it to ignite the gunpowder and set off the cannon.

With the wedding ceremony underway, I positioned myself near the front entrance of the church, ready to give my father the signal. Virtually everybody in Greenspond and Ship Island was out for the wedding. Those who were not in the church were standing around outside, waiting to see the bride and groom and catch a glimpse of the Lord Bishop, who was officiating at the wedding ceremony. Suddenly, the big moment arrived. The organist was playing, meaning that the formalities were over and the bridal party was about to emerge through the doors. Aiming my flashlight directly at the spot where my father was waiting, I flashed it three times. It was still light enough for me to see him put a torch to the gunpowder fuse, leading to the hole in the cannon breech, and ignite it.

The timing was perfect. At the precise moment that the newlyweds, followed by other members of the bridal party including several visiting clergymen and the Lord Bishop, stepped through the church door, all hell broke loose. The entire sky lit up as if a thousand firecrackers had exploded simultaneously. Taken completely by surprise, the bridal party and the onlookers standing around the churchyard stampeded, frantically seeking some place to take cover as wet, soggy caplin cascaded from the sky.

My father had been much too generous with the gunpowder when he loaded the cannon. What was intended to be a

minor blast turned out to be a deafening, earth-shaking explosion. Standing back a few feet from the church, I could not believe my eyes. What in the name of God is Father up to? I wondered. Is it the old cannon or are we having an earthquake? I started running towards Ship Island. Where, I wondered, did all the caplin come from?

I ran as quickly as my legs would carry me across the drawbridge. The cannon was lying on its side, still engulfed in smoke, with remnants of the oakum wad and the grass beneath the cannon still smouldering. My father was standing, in a state of shock, trying to figure out what had gone wrong. He knew from experience the quantity of gunpowder required to load a muzzle-loader. You simply poured gunpowder in the muzzle of the gun. The ram-rod used to tamp the gunpowder and the oakum wad down the breech were also used to measure the size of the load.

My father learned the hard way that loading a cannon was not that simple. He had no idea how much gunpowder to use, the extent to which it had to be tamped down, or the need to lash the cannon securely to the ground to keep it in place when the blast occurred. The fact that a bucket of caplin had been rammed down the cannon's breech added to the problem. The moment my father ignited the makeshift gunpowder fuse that led to the breech hole, the cannon left its base and hurled itself into the air, landing six feet away, where it lay smouldering like a spent firecracker.

My father needed no convincing that the cannon was overloaded. "But what was that stuff that shot out of the barrel and headed straight for the church?" he asked. When I told him it was soggy caplin, he was devastated.

As we walked away from the cannon, completely dejected and unsure if we dared to show our faces at the wedding reception, my father said, "I'll get that Bobby Carter for this."

Seven

A Tribute to a Born Adventurer

My older brother Allister was a born adventurer and risk taker, and he loved the sea. When he was sixteen, he and his friend Sylvester Meadus decided they wanted to see St. John's. Lacking the money to get there the conventional way, they decided to get there in a very unconventional way. They left Greenspond in the middle of the night in a 20-foot open motor boat, powered by a single-piston, make-and-break Acadia engine, and in weather that was subsequently described by the captain of the SS *Northern Ranger* as "not fit for man nor beast." They beat their way across Bonavista, Trinity and Conception Bays and arrived in St. John's several days later none the worse for their experience.

When the *Northern Ranger* arrived in Greenspond a couple of days later, Captain Jimmy Wheeler reported that he saw "the boys" as he was entering Catalina to seek shelter from the high winds and rough seas. "I could hardly believe my eyes," he said. "There we were seeking shelter from the storm, and there was this open motor boat with a couple of young fellows in it heading out across the bay as unconcerned as you would have it."

In the spring of 1939 Allister made an unscheduled trip to the ice onboard the SS *Neptune* with Captain Dominey. He tagged along behind the sealers, including my father, as they left Greenspond around the first of March to make their annual 50-mile trek to Gambo where they boarded the train for St. John's to "get their crop" and sign on for the seal hunt. In single file, the sealers would walk to Gambo, sometimes crawling on their hands and knees over thin bay ice, dragging their personal belongings behind them on hand-made slides.

The morning the *Neptune* sailed from St. John's, Allister was standing on the pier, wishing he was onboard. Shortly before it cast off, he got his wish. An officer on the vessel shouted to the few people still congregated on the pier, "Does anybody want a berth? We're a man short."

Even though he had only the clothes he stood in, Allister was not about to pass up the opportunity to go to the ice on the *Neptune*. He jumped onboard and scrambled to the ship's bridge where he signed on for the voyage. It is not difficult to imagine the surprised look on my father's face when he went on deck and saw his seventeen-year-old son leaning on the rail of the ship as it steamed out through the narrows.

Due to engine trouble and their inability to locate the main patch of seals, Allister's first and only trip to the ice was a dismal failure. That spring the crew of the *Neptune* suffered the ultimate humiliation; they did not make enough money to "clear their crop," the small line of credit provided by the vessel's owners for tobacco and a few other personal items. They were dropped off in their home communities when the hunt ended with not a penny.

Within weeks after World War II started in 1939, Allister tried to enlist in the Royal Navy. However, at seventeen, he was too young to enlist without my mother's consent, and she would not give it. In the spring of 1940, the British government commissioned a prominent Newfoundland master mariner, Captain Wesley Kean, to recruit young Newfoundland seamen to go overseas to man British merchant ships. Captain Kean's recruiting activities in Greenspond proved to be very successful. A number of young men, and some who were not so young, answered the call and were soon on their way to England to be assigned to British ships.

On a fine spring morning, led by the Salvation Army Band, the recruits paraded to the government wharf in

Greenspond. One of the youngest was Allister, carrying his cardboard suitcase and duffel bag. He had just turned eighteen. He and his friends boarded the passenger boat to Gambo and started out on a journey that for some would become a living hell from which they would never return.

Allister was a prodigious letter writer, and he never failed to inject a bit of humour in his letters to my mother. In one of his letters, he jokingly reminded my mother to ask Captain John Dominey to save him a berth to the ice on the *Neptune* when he returned home after the war. "Tell Captain Dominey," he wrote, "this time I will be sure to carry a change of underwear and some warm clothes."

In another letter to my mother written shortly after he arrived in England, he informed her he had signed on the *Lion Heart*, a pilot boat operating on the English Channel out of Dover. Not wanting to cause her worry, he tried to downplay the dangerous nature of the ship's assignment. "It's a wonderful job I got, hardly anything to do. The pay is good and the Captain is a great man. We are having a great time." What he did not tell my mother was that almost before he had time to unpack his bags, the *Lion Heart* was one of the many ships dispatched to the coast of France in early June, 1940 to take part in the evacuation of Dunkirk.

In a speech to the British House of Commons on June 4, 1940, Prime Minister Winston Churchill gave Members of Parliament a full briefing on the battle and subsequent evacuation of Dunkirk. He paid a special tribute to the men and ships that took part in the evacuation. Before a hushed chamber, Churchill said, "Using ships of all kinds, they gloriously retrieved more than 335,000 men, French and British, out of the jaws of death, and returned them to their native land. While we must be very careful not to assign to this deliverance the attributes of a victory—wars are not won by evacuations—there was a great victory inside this deliverance." Churchill concluded his speech with this final tribute:

"Every morn brought forth a noble chance, and every chance brought forth a noble knight."

On November 4, 1940, Allister wrote my mother again. The letter was postmarked Panama Canal. Allister was passing through on the SS *Loch Ranza*, a 10,000-ton freighter out of Glasgow, en route to England from British Columbia with a load of lumber on board. "I was some glad to get your letter and parcel before I left the other side," Allister wrote. "Thanks for the tobacco—it was some good to get a smoke of Bugler again."

He wrote again on December 13. This time the postmark was Glasgow. On the bottom of the last page, Allister wrote, "Well, mother, I had an experience a couple of weeks ago that I would not have missed for anything. On our way over, the ship I was on got torpedoed off the coast of Greenland. However, we got it to port all right. Three of us stuck with the ship and stayed with her until we were rescued."

The story of the torpedoing of the *Loch Ranza* and how it was towed to port with only the bridge above water (kept afloat by the buoyancy of the cargo) received front-page coverage in the Glasgow newspapers. When the torpedo hit, all but three members of the crew abandoned ship. My brother, the radio operator and the first mate were on the ship's bridge when the torpedo struck. The three of them decided to stay with the ship as it drifted helplessly, semi-submerged. It was sighted by a passing ship nine days later and towed to port in Scotland.

Allister's next ship was the SS *Neressa*, sailing between Great Britain, Canada and Newfoundland. On March 10, 1941, Allister wrote my mother from St. John's telling her that they were sailing the next day for England and that he was going to be made quartermaster on the return trip.

It seems that the *Neressa* was a vessel capable of above-average speed. It frequently crossed the U-boat infested North Atlantic without a convoy. It dared fate once too often. A week or so after it left St. John's, our minister, Rev. Fred Kirby, came to St. Stephen's School in Greenspond where my sister Kathleen and I were students. He told us the news. The SS *Neressa* had been torpedoed by a German U-boat. Allister was among the missing.

ALISTER CARTER
Brother of the author who was killed by enemy action in World War Two, off the Greenland coast.

One of the survivors who was on watch with my brother described what happened. He and Allister were leaning over the ship's rail when the torpedo hit. Both were thrown in the ocean where they clung to floating debris. The German U-boat surfaced as soon as its captain determined that their prey had been fatally hit. It remained on the surface for a couple of minutes. Suddenly there was a spray of machine-gun bullets aimed at the men in the water. Allister was killed instantly.

There is an epilogue to this story. In 1946, as they both turned 47, my father and mother became the parents of their fifth child, a boy (who is now a medical doctor practising in New Brunswick). They named him Allister.

Eight

The Blind Date

In the fall of 1947 I joined the Newfoundland Ranger Force, a law enforcement agency established by the Commission of Government in 1934 to enforce criminal law in rural areas of Newfoundland and Labrador. Modeled after the Royal Canadian Mounted Police and trained by RCMP personnel, the Newfoundland Ranger Force was also trained to provide an effective liaison between people in the outports and the government—which, during that period, governed without political accountability.

By the time I completed the various tests, including a strict medical examination, I was three months away from my eighteenth birthday, the required age for new recruits. I put off presenting my birth certificate to the Chief Ranger, Major E.L. Martin, for fear that he would reject my candidacy outright. Entry into the Ranger Force was not easy. Since the complement of the Force never numbered more than 72 men at any one time, entry usually took a long time. Therefore, I felt confident that if I was indeed accepted into the Rangers, I would by that time be well into my nineteenth year.

Unfortunately, it did not turn out that way. Three months before my eighteenth birthday, I was called into Ranger Headquarters in St. John's and told that I was accepted into the Force and would have to be available to commence training within a couple of days. However, they needed one more document to round out my file, and that was a copy of my birth certificate. I asked to speak with the Chief Ranger, Major Martin. I wanted to explain my situation to him personally. While I was in my eighteenth year, I was still three months away from my eighteenth birthday, so technically I was underage. Major Martin was very sympathetic. Since I was in good physical condition and met all their requirements in terms of height and weight, and since I would be going on nineteen by the time my training was completed, he was prepared to accept me into the Force with my parents' written consent.

Not to delay my departure for the training depot, Major Martin telephoned my mother while I was sitting in his office, to find out how she felt about my becoming a member of the Newfoundland Ranger Force. I had sensed all along that she was not overjoyed about me becoming a Ranger, so her reaction to Major Martin's telephone call was not totally unexpected. He explained to her that I would have to undergo six months training and by the time I was ready for my first assignment, I would be beyond the required age.

Mother's first question to the Major was, "Where are you going to send him when his training is completed?" He told her that I would have to go wherever I was sent. "Does that mean," she asked, "he might have to go to northern Labrador or some other isolated place like that?" Naturally, the Major answered in the affirmative. With that my mother asked to speak to me. She told me that she was not prepared to give her consent. "God only knows where they will end up sending you," she said. I thanked Major Martin for his consideration, apologized for any trouble I may have caused and walked out of his office feeling more dejected than I have ever felt in my entire life.

I often wonder what my life would have been like were it not for my mother's intervention. Following Confederation, the Newfoundland Ranger Force was disbanded and most of its members were absorbed into the Royal Canadian Mounted Police. More than likely, I would have exercised that option.

Never one to brood over disappointments or setbacks, I soon pursued other interests, one of which was destined to have an even greater impact on my life: my interest in a pretty young seventeen-year-old girl who had just gone to work as an office clerk at the Royal Stores on Water Street. Her name was Muriel Baker.

In its heyday, the Royal Stores was one of the largest and most prestigious retail outlets in the province. The MacPherson family, whose ancestors founded the business in 1895, had a better than average relationship with their workers, many of whom entered their employ in their youth and remained with the company until they retired. There was also an esprit de corps within the ranks of the workers themselves. They frequently engaged in extracurricular sports and social activities, the highlight of which was their annual spring dinner and dance.

My attendance at their 1947 dinner and dance as Muriel Baker's escort was made possible through the efforts of a third party. Since Muriel's date for the evening was unable to make it, one of her fellow workers, who was also an acquaintance of mine, suggested that she invite me as her escort. Subsequently, she and Muriel dropped into a certain restaurant where I frequently hung out. She introduced us and in a roundabout way suggested that I be Muriel's date.

I am not sure what the accumulated compound interest would be on a five-dollar investment negotiated fifty years ago, but that is the amount I still owe Muriel for the price of the ticket she had bought before we met. Whenever I offered to reimburse her for the price of the ticket, she refused and suggested that I pay her later. Eventually, it was forgotten and the debt was never paid. Over the years I have taken considerable good-natured ribbing from Muriel over the fact that I still owe her the five dollars for the ticket, plus interest.

From that first date on May 20, 1947, evolved a friendship and a love that has endured over fifty years and is still strong. We were married in 1949 in Gower Street United Church. Muriel was still in her teens and I had just turned twenty. Our first son, Roger, was born on our first wedding anniversary. Two years later our first daughter, Donna Lynn, arrived and then David, Paul, Glenn, Bonnie, Gregory and Susan came along. Over a thirteen-year period, Muriel gave birth to eight healthy, bright, good-looking children who have since blessed us with fourteen equally healthy, bright and good-looking grandchildren.

Muriel's parents lived on Goodridge Street in a working-class area of St. John's known locally as Rabbittown. They were both born and raised on Random Island and in many respects had a lot in common with my parents. Allan and Laura Baker were extremely hard-working, independent, honest people who not only preached the Golden Rule, but practised it on a daily basis.

In his poem, "An Essay On Man" the English poet Alexander Pope, described an honest man as "the noblest work of God." Muriel's father, Allan Baker, a master builder and construction foreman, fit that description to a T. He was one of the most honest and honourable men I have ever known. His temperament and philosophy of life were refreshing. He was one of the few people I have ever met who was literally incapable of lying, cheating or gossip-mongering. In every sense of the word, Allan Baker was an exemplary human being. Muriel's mother, Laura Baker, was one of the most remarkable women I have ever known. An interesting conversationalist, she was remarkably well-informed and right up until her sudden passing in 1998, maintained a keen interest in current events. Her entire life was one of giving of herself and helping others. I would jokingly refer to her as the Mother Teresa of Rabbittown. She gave away more free meals and befriended more people than any other person I have known. It did not matter who or what you were; when you visited the Baker home your chances of getting away without a cup of "steeped tea" and a piece of homemade cake were pretty slim.

Muriel, the eldest of nine children, inherited most of her parents attributes. There is no greater compliment I could pay her.

So it was that chance played an important part in what would become of me. Just as one career choice was put aside, a blind date brought into my life the kind of relationships that enrich a lifetime.

Nine

Listening in on the Great Debate

In the mid-1940s, when Major Peter J. Cashin started his campaign for a return of Responsible Government and lambasted the Commission of Government in a weekly broadcast over radio station VOCM, it was music to my ears. It did not matter where I was or what I was doing. A few minutes before nine o'clock on Saturday night, I would drop everything and run home. I would sit at the kitchen table with my parents and usually several like-minded neighbours and anxiously wait to hear the "Banks of Newfoundland," the ditty used by the radio station to introduce the fiery Major Cashin.

In 1948 Newfoundland was a country in search of a political identity. Shortly after I left my native Greenspond to live in St. John's, the newly elected members of the National Convention were about to take their seats in the Colonial Building to commence debate on the constitutional future of Newfoundland. Despite the growing restlessness that had developed in Newfoundland with the Commission of Government, and the fact that a great many Newfoundlanders would not be sorry to see it go, there was no unanimous voice as to what should take its place.

From the outset, there were two dominant characters in the National Convention, Joseph R. Smallwood and Major Peter J. Cashin. Both were the best-known advocates of their respective causes and were looked upon as the leaders of the main opposing factions, union with Canada and restoration of Responsible Government. But Smallwood shrewdly sensed the necessity of a wider audience than summaries of the proceedings could procure through press and radio reports. Shortly after the Convention convened, microphones made their appearance in the chamber. The government-run broadcasting station, probably with a prod from Smallwood, decided to record and air the proceedings in full. As things turned out it was a decision that changed the course of Newfoundland history. It undoubtedly had a tremendous impact on the people of Newfoundland and was the beginning of the most dramatic period in our long, turbulent history. It was also a boon for Smallwood. With the proceedings of the National Convention broadcast night after night at full length, when Smallwood was ready to establish the case for Confederation, he had the whole country for his audience.

Having developed an oratorical style that appealed to what he called the "ragged arsed artillery," Smallwood, elected to the Convention as a champion of Confederation, had a field day. Converted to the Confederation cause while operating a piggery at Gander, he was now possessed by a messianic mission. A born crusader, whose life had been largely committed to the pursuit of lost causes, Smallwood was in his forty-sixth year when his proverbial ship finally came in. Always forceful and aggressively articulate, Smallwood had spent his whole life preparing himself for an opportunity if and when it arrived. He found it in the National Convention and his advocacy of Confederation.

Major Peter Cashin, the foremost anti-confederate, was also a crusader in search of a cause. Peter Cashin was not without considerable experience in the art of politics. Between 1923 and 1932 he was elected and re-elected three times and, for a time, served as Minister of Finance in the Liberal administration of Sir Richard Squires. As an orator and politician, Cashin had few equals in Newfoundland during that period.

Determined to rid Newfoundland of the Commission of Government, categorized by Cashin in his weekly broadcasts as "stool pigeons for the British Dominions Office in London," he goaded and tormented the Commission of Government mercilessly. His language was as belligerent as it was inflammatory. He was a born rabble-rouser, of whom a local wag once said, "He could incite a riot with the reading of the twenty-third psalm!"

Initially, Cashin made two or three speeches over the government-controlled radio station VONF, but his relationship with it was short-lived. He had a falling out with the management, whom he described as "flunkies for the English Commissioners." He accused the management of censoring his speeches "beyond recognition" on instructions from the Commission of Government that, he said, would stop at nothing to cover their many misdeeds.

In the mid-1940s, there were only two radio stations in Newfoundland: VONF, owned and operated by the government; and VOCM, owned by the Butler family. Prevented from venting his spleen on the government station, Cashin went to the owners of VOCM. They agreed to give him thirty minutes of air time every Saturday night at nine o'clock.

I missed none of Cashin's radio broadcasts. Proudly proclaiming that he was an "unrepentant advocate of a simple restoration of Responsible Government," he argued that under the 1933 agreement which ended self-government, a pledge had been given Newfoundlanders that as soon as their difficulties were overcome and their government was again self-supporting, Responsible Government would be restored, if requested. Cashin's argument was simple: "Since we are now in the black and have 40 million dollars to our credit in the bank, which means we are self-supporting, give us back Responsible Government without further delay."

The simplicity of his message, his flamboyant style, and the provocative charges he made provided the best entertainment on the air, even for non-believers. At that time I was anything but a non-believer. I believed very strongly in what Major Cashin was saying and trying to do. In retrospect, the situation was remarkably ironic. As scores of small countries, which later emerged as powerful Third World countries, were fighting and dying for independence, we Newfoundlanders couldn't wait to surrender ours. Like sheep, we rushed head-long into a political union on terms that were not properly negotiated or debated.

I was equally enthusiastic about another radio program aired nightly on VONF, "The Barrelman," featuring Joseph R. Smallwood. While Newfoundlanders were growing in-creasingly restless in the political vacuum of the Commission of Government era, Smallwood told stories of the greatness of former leaders and the daring exploits and achievements of Newfoundlanders at home and abroad. In the process of carrying out the program's aim— instilling pride in our people and "making Newfoundland better known to New-foundlanders"—Smallwood was also making himself better known to Newfoundlanders. This later proved to be very beneficial for him and the cause of union with Canada.

While most teenagers were taking their girlfriends to a movie or a hockey game, I talked my girlfriend, Muriel Baker, into accompanying me to the National Convention. We sat for countless hours in the gallery of the old House of Assembly in the Colonial Building, engrossed in the debates taking place. I followed the proceedings assiduously and, in the process, acquired considerable respect and admiration for some of its key players, including Smallwood, Cashin and my political idol, Kenneth M. Brown.

Unfortunately, Brown's contribution to the debate was short-lived. On October 26, 1946 he collapsed on the floor of the National Convention while making a strong anti-confed-erate speech and had to be carried from the building on a stretcher. He had suffered a paralytic stroke and never again returned to the Assembly.

Within a short while, the battle lines were firmly drawn between the adherents of restoration of Responsible Government and those who supported Confederation with Canada. Even though my family were ardent supporters of union with Canada, I would have voted for a return of Responsible Government had I been old enough to vote. Although only marginally involved with the issue, I had the gut feeling that while the ultimate outcome of Confederation might be in Newfoundland's best interest, the methods being used to achieve it were wrong. In retrospect, while I am far from convinced that union with Canada was in Newfoundland's best long-term interest, I *am* certain that the process used to bring it about was wrong. The final terms and conditions under which union was consummated should have been negotiated by a sovereign, elected Government and subsequently voted on in a general election.

As we celebrate the fiftieth anniversary of our union with Canada, Newfoundlanders and Labradorians are still on the bottom rung of Canada's social and economic ladder.

Into the Fray

Ten

Politics and Religion: Beyond the Labels

I have spent most of my life in politics. I have been elected and re-elected to the three levels of government eleven times. Despite this, I have never taken party labels too seriously. Nor have I blindly followed a party leader or pretended to be loyal to a political party or leader in which I lacked confidence. Since there are no substantive philosophical differences between the Conservative and Liberal parties in this country, and these are the only political parties in which I feel comfortable, I am more influenced by their respective leaders and the calibre of the people they attract than by traditional party labels.

Politically, I have always been guided by the principle that no political party or leader has a monopoly on honesty, commitment or the will to do what is right. I have always supported the party and the leader whom I consider to be the most honest, have the strongest commitment to the people, and possess the most determination to do what is right.

In 1968 when Trudeaumania was sweeping the country and the fortunes of the Liberal Party were at an all-time high, I literally walked away from the Liberal Party and became a member of the Progressive Conservative Party. I was attracted to the Conservative Party, not because there was any appreciable difference in the traditional political philosophies of the two parties, but because I believed that the Conservative leader, Robert Stanfield, was best able to bring about the changes I thought necessary to make Confederation more meaningful to Canadians. I felt that this was

Taken outside Government House in 1975 after being sworn in as
Minister of Fisheries in the Moores Cabinet. In the picture from left to
right; John Lundrigan, Dr. Tom Farrell, Walter Carter.

especially important for those of us who lived in the so-called
disadvantaged regions of Canada. I am no less convinced
today than I was in 1968 that, had he been elected, Stanfield
would have been one of the best Prime Ministers this country
ever had.

I do not possess the kind of religious and political bias
that unwavering allegiance to a party or denomination seems
to require. Politically, I have always considered myself to be a
cross between a right-wing Liberal and a left-wing Conservative, which places me in the middle of the political spectrum.

From the standpoint of my church affiliation, I am a
Christian. While I am a Protestant by birth and was brought
up in the Anglican faith, I feel just as much at home sitting in
a pew in a Roman Catholic Church as I do sitting in a pew in
an Anglican Church, or for that matter any other Protestant
Church. I agree with George Bernard Shaw: "There is only
one religion, though there are a hundred versions of it."

I never ceased to be amused by people who follow the
Benjamin Disraeli dogma, "Damn your principles! Stick to

your party!" In my view, far too many politicians and would-be politicians subscribe to that creed. I am not and never was a party person. The public figures I admire most, nationally and provincially, are opposites in their respective political affiliations. From a Newfoundland perspective, I consider Joe Smallwood the greatest Premier since Confederation. I also believe that Frank Duff Moores, the man who defeated Smallwood in 1971, will be remembered by fair and open-minded students of the post-Confederation history of Newfoundland and Labrador as a truly great Premier. Smallwood and Moores were on opposite sides of the political spectrum, but were nonetheless outstanding Newfoundlanders and Premiers.

From a national perspective, as a Canadian since 1949, I believe that John G. Diefenbaker and Lester B. Pearson, political adversaries and leaders of parties of different political stripes, were Canada's most outstanding Prime Ministers.

Always interested in politics but more interested in people and process than in parties, as a young man I was open to the opportunity to become politically involved. Such an opportunity came my way in 1951.

Eleven

My First Campaign

In the 1951 provincial general election, I campaigned in the dual district of St. John's East for Liberal candidates Bill Ryan and William J. Ashley. My involvement began with my search for a very different kind of opportunity.

About that time, Smallwood and his newly appointed Director-General of Economic Development for Newfoundland, Dr. Alfred Valdmanis, seemed to be having considerable success in their efforts to entice European industrialists to establish factories in Newfoundland. Smallwood's "develop or perish" policy appeared to be paying off. Scarcely a week passed when he was not in the news announcing a new industry for Newfoundland. In one of his press statements, he indicated that as part of his government's economic development program, young Newfoundlanders would be recruited and sent to Europe, where they would be trained by parent companies for management jobs in the new plants they planned to establish here.

Like most Newfoundlanders, I was caught up completely in the excitement and expectations of the post-Confederation era. The prospect of getting in on the ground floor of the Smallwood government's new economic development program excited me tremendously. Consequently, I decided to meet with the Premier who was also the Member for the House of Assembly for my native Bonavista North, and make him aware of my interest in the training program he had referred to in the news media.

My meeting with Smallwood took place in his office in

Canada House on Circular Road where the Premier maintained a residence and an office. It was a couple of days after
the 1951 provincial election call. Smallwood was noted for his
work schedule, which frequently included press conferences
and Cabinet meetings at all hours of the night. Late one
evening I drove past Canada House. Observing that the lights
were still on, and several cars were parked in the driveway, I
decided to visit him.

Minutes after being admitted to the outside waiting area
by Mrs. Smallwood, I was ushered into the Premier's office,
where he was having a few parting words with several people
whom I recognized as Members of his Cabinet. Two Ministers, the Attorney General and the Minister of Labour, stayed
behind and remained seated. Obviously their meeting with
the Premier was not over. This left me in a quandary as to
what I should do. Smallwood was beckoning me to enter and
take a seat while still engaged in conversation with the two
Ministers.

The moment I introduced myself and told him where I
was from, Smallwood immediately launched into the history
of the Greenspond Carters. He told me that Captain Peter
Carter, a well-known sealing captain, was the first person in
Bonavista North to join the Confederate cause when it was
launched in the late 1940s. Smallwood also knew my father.
He talked at length about the old building that was owned by
my family in Greenspond and used as a trap loft. It was
originally owned by Smallwood's grandfather, David Smallwood, in which he operated a general business and fishery
supply store in the latter half of the 1800s. It was during that
period that David Smallwood was said to have flown the
Confederate flag on the premises during the 1869 election on
the issue of Confederation and was forced by the residents to
take it down. Smallwood told me that on one of his visits to
Greenspond during the Confederation campaign, he visited
the old store and removed several artifacts, including the

Sunlight Soap sign that was still attached to the front of the
building below the window, and which bore his grandfather's
name.

What a strange situation this is! I thought. Here I am, a
twenty-one-year-old unknown, who walked in off the street
and is now, at eleven o'clock at night, sitting in the Premier's
office and interrupting a meeting between the Premier and
two of his most important Ministers, and I still haven't had a
chance to tell him why I am here. While the two Ministers
were trying hard to appear interested in what was being said,
for the next fifteen or twenty minutes Smallwood continued

talking about the Carter family, Greenspond, and the over-whelming support he received there for Confederation.

Finally, he got around to asking me what I wanted. Feeling somewhat sheepish about having to discuss personal business in the presence of the two Cabinet Ministers, I told Smallwood that I was encouraged by the success he was having in attracting new industry to Newfoundland and that I wanted to be involved. I reminded him of a statement he had made earlier to the media about sending young New-foundlanders to Europe to be trained for jobs in the new industries that were being established. I told him that I was interested.

He assured me that I would be given "very careful consid-eration" when the time came to select the people who would be sent to Germany for training. He told the Minister of Labour, who was still patiently waiting to get on with his business, to be sure to remind him of my interest when the time came to select the people to be trained.

As I was leaving his office, Smallwood called me back and asked me if I would be interested in taking part in the upcoming election campaign. Within seconds of my telling him I would be delighted to be involved, he was on the telephone to William J. Ashley, who was about to be an-nounced as a candidate in the dual riding of St. John's East. He told Ashley that he wanted me to be involved in the St. John's East election campaign.

A few hours after Ashley's candidacy was announced the following day, I was sitting in his office, discussing the role I would play in the upcoming campaign. It was agreed that my job would be to arrange meetings for the candidates in the rural part of the district, which extended to Pouch Cove and Bauline. Using a car with a public address system mounted on its roof, I would blitz the outlying communities and drum up interest in the meetings which, during the last week of the campaign, were planned for every night. It was also agreed that, weather permitting, we would arrange outdoor after-noon meetings as well.

One such afternoon meeting was planned for Pouch Cove, and Premier Smallwood would be in attendance. It was planned to have people assemble in an open area in the centre of the community. The Premier would then speak to them over the public address system attached to the roof of my car.

I spent the entire day driving around the Pouch Cove and Bauline area, announcing the meeting and its star attraction, Premier Smallwood. Once the word was out that "Joey" would be there, it took little effort to drum up interest. By early afternoon the place was alive. Flags were flying, some on makeshift flagpoles and, hours before the meeting was sched-uled to commence, people started coming from all direc-tions, including the children who were let out of school an hour early for the occasion. Trying not to be too conspicuous, a number of old fishermen were standing around with their muzzle-loaders by their sides, primed and prepared to give Joey a rousing, traditional Pouch Cove welcome. Unlike the other rural communities in St. John's East, Pouch Cove and Bauline were Liberal to the core, and they were not reticent in showing their political colours.

At the appropriate time, I met the Premier's car a short distance outside Pouch Cove and led it, with music blaring over the loudspeaker, to the centre of the community where the crowd was assembled. As we approached the meeting place, I knew that my efforts had paid off. The place was crowded, people were cheering, the children were waving signs or anything else they could get their hands on, and several fishermen were firing off muzzle-loaders.

I don't know if it was fate, impulsiveness or plain gall, but that brief encounter with Premier Smallwood in Pouch Cove on that sunny, November afternoon, along with the events that were to follow, changed my whole life. It started me on a political career that lasted for thirty-five years. During that time I was elected and re-elected eleven times, which is a record in Newfoundland politics. I established other records, too. I sat in the House of Assembly with every Premier since Confederation, including Smallwood, Moores, Peckford, Rideout, Wells and Tobin. No other Newfoundlander, living or dead, can make that claim. I was Minister of Fisheries longer than any of my predecessors, serving in that capacity for nine years under three Premiers in both Tory and Liberal administrations. I was also elected Deputy Mayor of St. John's, which was predominantly Tory, while representing a Liberal northern district in the House of Assembly. I was elected three times to the Canadian House of Commons and, in the process, outlasted all my political contemporaries.

The time came to introduce the Premier to the people assembled in Pouch Cove that afternoon. However, the person assigned the responsibility lost his nerve and, at the last minute, handed me the microphone and told me to "do the honours." Having spent all day driving around the communities, using the public address system, I had no difficulty performing the task. My introduction of the Premier received such a warm response from the crowd that I got carried away and, before handing the microphone over to him, decided to make a short political speech of my own.

After the meeting, we were invited to the Grouchy home in Pouch Cove, where we were treated to a meal of corned beef and cabbage. All during the meal, the people at the table were having a bit of good-natured fun with me about my speech and the reaction it had received from the crowd. Smallwood predicted that someday I would be a member of the House of Assembly, maybe even Premier. Despite the bantering, he was obviously impressed, because later that night I received a telephone call from Liberal Headquarters, informing me that the Premier liked the way I had arranged things in Pouch Cove that afternoon and wanted me to accompany him, with the sound car, on a tour of the north-east coast. We would be leaving from the Premier's Circular Road residence early the next morning. I was told to come prepared for a three- or four-day trip, and that I should follow the same format I had followed in Pouch Cove.

The next three days were spent campaigning in communities in Conception, Trinity and Bonavista Bays with the candidates for the districts. As we approached a community, I kept well ahead of the Premier's car, announcing over the public address system his impending arrival. Using either an electronic bull horn or the public address system on my car, Smallwood would give a rousing speech to the people who gathered around, extol the virtues of the Liberal candidate for that particular area, shake hands with people standing on the side of the roads, and move on to another community.

The people's response to Smallwood in all the communities we visited was phenomenal. They couldn't seem to get enough of him. With the Confederation issue still fresh in their minds, and the prosperity they were enjoying as a result of the social benefits they were receiving from Ottawa, including old age pensions, veteran's pensions and the baby bonus, Joey was still their hero.

We concluded the tour with a public meeting in Harbour Main on Saturday night, with the candidates for the dual district of Harbour Main-Bell Island, Philip J. Lewis and Addison Bown. This would be the end of the 1951 election campaign. Monday was polling day.

After the meeting, we were invited to the Lewis family home in Holyrood where the four of us, including Smallwood, the two candidates, and myself ate a delicious meal prepared by Mrs. Lewis. We then sat around the fireplace, listening to Smallwood as he told some of the most interesting political stories I have ever heard.

With the campaign over and the Liberal Party heading for another sweeping victory, it was time to relax and reflect on the present campaign and past elections. Smallwood was in a very special mood. One story led to another and, before we knew it, we were being treated to a detailed account of the events leading up to Confederation. We sat in front of the living room fireplace until dawn, completely enthraled as Smallwood told us the "inside" story of the fight for Confederation: the intrigue of the backroom politics, the broken promises, the deals that were made and the betrayals.

I have read almost everything there is to read about that period in Newfoundland's history. But Smallwood's reminiscences that evening gave me a far greater insight into what actually took place during that period than anything I have read since. My only regret is that I was unable to record it for posterity.

The sun was coming up over the hills as we headed for home on the Conception Bay Highway. Perhaps it was the lingering excitement of the evening before, or an omen of things to come, but it was the most beautiful sunrise I have ever seen.

Immediately after the election, I was offered a position in the Premier's Office at Canada House. I spent the next eight years there observing Smallwood and participating in the most exciting period in Newfoundland's political history.

Twelve

The IWA Strike

In my eight years in the Premier's Office, one of the most turbulent events I witnessed was the International Woodworkers of America (IWA) strike of 1959. The strike caused enormous strife in the province's logging industry. Against the wishes of both paper companies operating in the province, the IWA was certified as the bargaining agent for the loggers supplying the paper mills in Corner Brook and Grand Falls.

The leader of the certification drive was H. Landon Ladd.

Born in Vancouver, Ladd was president for Eastern Canada of the International Woodworkers of America when he led the organizing drive among Newfoundland loggers. A hard-nosed trade unionist, in 1956 Ladd began a concerted effort to convince loggers employed by the Anglo-Newfoundland-Development Company to join his union. Living conditions in logging camps at that time were far from adequate. It did not take long for Ladd to convince the loggers employed by Bowaters and the A.N.D. Company that they had nothing to lose by joining the IWA. It was certified as the bargaining agent for the loggers in 1957 and 1958. After attempts to negotiate a contract proved fruitless, Ladd called a strike against the A.N.D. Company on December 31, 1958, and what followed was the most divisive, strife-ridden period in Newfoundland's labour history.

The management of the Grand Falls Mill warned that a strike might cripple the company and force it to shut down permanently. Yet, when the IWA polled its members, 98 percent voted to strike. Warnings of this nature (especially by management) were seldom taken seriously by union heads. However, in Newfoundland the strike vote was being taken seriously—even, it seemed, by Premier Smallwood himself. The issue was not whether the paper companies could afford an increase in the cost of their wood. It was simply a question of whether or not the loggers would be allowed to have the IWA as their bargaining agent. Their right of choice was important to them.

The strike lasted until the union was finally decertified by the House of Assembly on March 6, 1959. Smallwood intervened when it became apparent that the company was virtually beaten. With no previous hint of his sympathies in the matter, he went on the radio on the night of February 12 to denounce the IWA as a vicious invasion force from the mainland guilty of starting "not a strike but a civil war."

"How dare these outsiders," said he, "come into this decent Christian province and by such desperate methods try to seize control of our province's most important industry. How dare they come in here and spread their black poison of class hatred and bitter, bigoted prejudice. How dare they come into this province amongst decent God-fearing people and let loose the dirt and filth and poison of the last four weeks."

Smallwood's speech was nothing less than a declaration of war. He accused the IWA leadership of being a front for Jimmy Hoffa's Teamsters union—whom he described as "pimps, panderers, white slavers, murderers, embezzlers, extortioners, manslaughterers and dope peddlers." In a speech in the House of Assembly, he made the same accusations, connecting Landon Ladd and the IWA with the Mafia and other organized crime in the United States. Anti-IWA feeling began to run rampant in the province.

A few days later, with the battle lines clearly drawn, Smallwood established a headquarters at the Staff House in

Grand Falls from which he waged a well-planned campaign against the IWA and H. Landon Ladd. He also launched a campaign to organize a new loggers union to replace the much-maligned IWA.

With the unanimous support of the Newfoundland Legislature and the province's news media, Smallwood spared no effort to break the strike and send the IWA and its leader packing. He offered the loggers a government-sponsored union that could bypass the lengthy Labour Relations Board certification process. He would certify it himself by passing a law in the House of Assembly.

Smallwood temporarily relieved me of my duties in the Premier's Office and took me to Grand Falls with him to help organize the new union. Under his direction, a number of us travelled the area from White Bay to Trinity Bay, where 98% of the loggers employed with the Grand Falls mill lived. The purpose of the trip was to gather information, to find out what they were thinking. "Keep your mouths shut and your eyes and ears open," Smallwood said, "and find out what the people are saying about the IWA and the strike." The other members of the team assigned to that task included Max Lane, (MHA for White Bay North), St. John's Lawyer Bill Adams, Greg O'Grady (a former manager of the Unemployment Insurance Commission), Bill Smallwood and Elmer Vaters—-whose father was head of the Pentecostal Assemblies in Newfoundland.

Greg O'Grady and I were assigned the area from Grand Falls to Gambo. For ten days we visited the home of every known logger in the area, listening to what they were saying and discreetly promoting the idea of organizing a new loggers union to replace the IWA.

At night we would all meet with Smallwood in his Staff House suite for a debriefing. As we compared notes, we agreed that the response we were getting from the loggers and the public in the areas visited was encouraging. However,

Smallwood was not content to deal in generalities. He wanted to know precisely whom we met, how they reacted to our visit, and what they said. He had to be sure where he stood with the people, especially the loggers, before he brought things to a head.

Satisfied that public opinion and a significant number of loggers were on side, Smallwood decided to make his move. He announced that a public meeting would be held in the Grand Falls town hall on March 4 for the purpose of launching a new union to replace the IWA. He urged all loggers to desert the IWA and become members of the new union. Said Smallwood, "It is the duty of every Newfoundlander to stop the IWA in their tracks—to boot the IWA out of Newfoundland."

The strike attracted an astonishing level of national and international press coverage. Media people from all over North America converged on Grand Falls in anticipation of the big showdown between Smallwood and Landon Ladd predicted to take place at the meeting.

Smallwood had gotten a standing ovation in the House of Assembly a few days previous, when he introduced a resolution condemning the actions of the IWA as a "stumbling block to the pulp and paper industry in Newfoundland and a danger to the public interest." Subsequently, he had the Legislature pass two pieces of legislation that he described as emergency laws. The first decertified the IWA in Newfoundland. The second gave the government power to dissolve any union if its' officers had been convicted of certain crimes including white slavery, dope peddling, manslaughter or embezzlement.

Apparently, this was the only time in Canada that a union was named and abolished by law.

The two laws aroused shock and indignation throughout Canada. Overtures by the Diefenbaker Conservative government to the Lieutenant-Governor—-to withhold royal assent until they could examine the constitutionality of the laws—- were ignored. The Lieutenant-Governor signed the two bills into law immediately.

The position of the IWA was hopeless. Even if the union pushed the company into negotiating an agreement, it would have no legal effect. As an outlawed union the strikers had two options; accept defeat and return to work, or defy the law and go down fighting. They chose the latter.

On March 11, several hundred loggers and their families blocked the main road in Badger in defiance of the police order to disperse. Marching three abreast and carrying nightsticks, a column of 75 police officers waded into the group of striking loggers, desperately fighting to restore order to the inherent chaos of the crowd.

The riot lasted for twenty minutes. When it was over, a dozen or so strikers were arrested and others were nursing lacerations and sore limbs. Constable William Moss, a member of the Newfoundland Constabulary, lay on the snow-covered ground, fatally injured.

Smallwood's tactic was to do what he did best—let loose his oratorical and persuasive powers in the forum of a public meeting. On the day of the meeting, Grand Falls was swarming with reporters and cameramen from every major news outlet in Canada. It was also swarming with loggers, as buses converged on Grand Falls filled to capacity. RCMP street patrols were strengthened early in the day as hundreds of spectators congregated in front of the town hall and the new union office directly across from it.

By the time the meeting was ready to begin, there was not even standing room available in the hall. Since the stakes were high for the IWA leadership, those of us who were close to the situation did not take too lightly the rumours circulating for days in the Grand Falls area that IWA supporters would be encouraged by Ladd and his associates to infiltrate the meeting and at the appropriate moment "put her up." However, the moment Smallwood appeared on the platform, we knew that our fears in that regard were groundless. Before he got a chance to utter a word, the place went wild. Whenever he tried to speak, the cheering of the crowd and the applause made it impossible for him to be heard. Finally, when the audience had settled down and with Smallwood in complete control of the situation, he proceeded to deliver the most rousing speech I have ever heard him make.

As an orator, Smallwood was in a class all to himself. He had a unique way of working up a crowd. When he got them worked up, he would invite comment from people in the audience, especially when he knew they were on his side. Since the meeting was being broadcast live right across Canada, Smallwood wanted to be sure that the rest of the country got an earful. As he was winding up his speech and the excitement was at its peak, he invited people from the audience to come to the platform and say a few words. He would start by asking them their name, where they were from and what brought them to Grand Falls.

In all but one case it worked extremely well. The people Smallwood invited to the platform said all the things he wanted other Canadians to hear. Proudly, they would say; "We're here sir to join your new union and give that feller Landon Ladd his walking ticket."

The last person called to the platform was a logger from New World Island. "Now my good man, what is your name and where are you from?" Smallwood asked.

The logger gave his name and said he was from New World Island.

"And what are you doing here today?" asked Smallwood.

"I'm here, Mr. Smallwood sir, to join your new union and give them IWA fellers the boot," he replied.

"So, you're from New World Island, are you. That's a fair distance away isn't it—how did you get here?" questioned Smallwood. "Did you come by bus or did you get a ride with a friend?"

To which the logger replied, "No sir, I come in on me bike." Smallwood was beaming. He instinctively knew he had the makings of a good, human interest story, tailor-made for national consumption. "Speak into the microphones so the rest of Canada will hear you," he told the logger as he tried to nudge him closer to the rostrum. "Now then, do you mean to tell the people in this hall and the millions who are listening to us this very moment right across Canada that you came all the way from New World Island, which is a good 80 miles north of here, on a bicycle, to join the new union?" said Smallwood.

"No sir," replied the logger, "I'd be telling ye a lie if I said I come all the way on me bike. I had a misfartune. I fell off her on the hill this side of Narris's Harm and I slided about 200 feet on me arse."

Thus Smallwood gave the Canadian public all he wanted them to hear, and something a little less planned.

The IWA opposition did not materialize. After Constable Moss's death, Ladd realized that public opinion in Newfoundland had turned against him and his union and, on March 20, he told the loggers to return to work to save their jobs.

Thirteen

Youth, Energy and Vision

As a rule, municipal election campaigns in St. John's were mundane, routine affairs—-that is, elections prior to the one held in 1961. The candidates made their usual personal contacts, handed out postcard-size handbills, attended a few funerals, took part in the annual Wesley Church radio auction over station VOWR a few days before polling day, and left it at that. Large posters and radio and television advertising were unheard of. Most of the candidates conducted word-of-mouth, personalized campaigns. A few days before polling day, the more aggressive ones had a few thirty-second blurbs on radio, and placed small, single-column ads in the daily newspapers.

The right to vote in a St. John's municipal election prior to 1975 was extended only to residential and commercial property owners, one vote for each property you owned and always on the condition that all municipal taxes were paid in full. Administrators of estates, including lawyers and trust company officials who managed properties for absentee landlords, had the right to cast a vote for each of the properties they managed. It was a neat, cosy arrangement which made it difficult for an outsider to penetrate the municipal electoral system, unless you had the blessing of the city's establishment.

Most of the people who challenged the system lacked either the political know-how, the money or the credibility to pose a serious threat to the sitting councillors. Occasionally, there would be an upset. But generally speaking, incumbents who looked after their downtown corporate friends and were known to be trustworthy could always count on the establishment and the old boys' network to keep them in office. As far as the establishment was concerned, it was a case of electing the devil you knew as opposed to the one you didn't.

I decided during the summer of 1961 to be a candidate in the upcoming municipal election, slated for November 14, even though I knew I would be able to count on neither moral support nor financial contributions towards the campaign from the St. John's establishment.

I discussed my possible candidacy with a few close friends and leaders of certain interest groups within the city, including the St. John's Home Builders Association, and was encouraged by their reaction. A few days after the Labour Day weekend, I issued a press release announcing my candidacy.

By the time the campaign was underway in earnest, twelve other St. John's residents, all of whom were well known in various activities in the city, had announced their intention to seek a seat on the six-member council.

The most promising of the lot was Bill Adams, a 38-year-old St. John's lawyer. The offspring of a solid St. John's working-class family, Adams was extremely capable and likable. When he was in his mid-twenties, he quit his job as labourer at the Newfoundland Railway and enroled in Dalhousie Law School. His personal attributes, along with his involvement in various charitable and service organizations, made him a first-rate candidate for any office in St. John's.

Adam's candidacy in the 1961 municipal election was the start of a successful career in public life. First elected as Deputy Mayor of St. John's, he went on to become its Mayor. In 1962 he was elected a member of the House of Assembly, and was subsequently appointed to the Smallwood Cabinet. He ended his career in public life as a Justice of the Newfoundland Supreme Court.

There were other well-known St. John's residents running for a council seat in that election, including Jim Fagan, Ank Murphy, Robert Barrett and Albert Andrews. Murphy, Barrett and Andrews had earlier tried unsuccessfully to get a seat on council. Like myself, Fagan was making his first bid for a seat. In 1949 he had run for the Liberal Party in the riding of St. John's East with Geoff Carnell. However, despite their personal popularity, both he and Carnell were defeated by Tories Frank Fogwill and John Higgins.

There would have to be at least one new face on council after the 1961 municipal election, to fill the seat left vacant by the death of Joe Fitzgibbon, who had served on the council since 1949. As the campaign heated up, the front-runners within the challenger ranks started to emerge. Having already agreed among themselves over coffee at McMurdo's or a glass of sherry at the City Club that the incumbents would be re-elected, members of the establishment were trying to decide which one of the newcomers could be trusted to fill the vacant seat. No doubt Adams was their choice as a suitable replacement for Fitzgibbon. As a downtown lawyer, Adams was in tune with members of the business establishment, sharing their interest in several high-profile community projects.

My interest in politics had started at a young age, and it intensified during the years I spent in the Premier's Office.

In that eight-year period, Newfoundlanders and Labradorians went to the polls six times, three times each to elect a provincial government and a federal government. For me, it was too good to be true. I had the opportunity to be around a master politician and become totally immersed in what had become my first love, politics. I learned a lot about politics: how to organize and run a campaign and, most importantly, how to keep getting re-elected.

Smallwood was the consummate politician. He took politics seriously and would never go out of his way to avoid a spirited political fight. Even though there were many people around him who were quite capable of organizing a political campaign, the moment an election was called, he was in charge and would personally oversee even minute details. Once the battle lines were drawn, he pulled out all the stops to win. His philosophy was: "In politics there is no prize for placing second."

One of the many things I learned from Smallwood was the importance of the recognition factor. All other things being equal, the more recognizable a candidate was, the better his chances were of getting elected. That is why Smallwood always placed great emphasis on signs and posters as a means of achieving constant visibility.

In the period leading up to an election campaign in Newfoundland, sign painting was our fastest-growing industry. One of the most successful sign-painting companies in the province was owned by a friend of mine who was also a prominent member of the Liberal Party, Hal Austin. The Austin Advertising Agency was professional in every sense of the word. Unlike most of the sign-painting companies that emerged during election campaigns and fizzled the moment the election was over, the Austin Advertising Agency was well established and remained financially sound even without the infusion of money generated by election campaigns.

Shortly after announcing my intention to be a candidate in 1961, I arranged a meeting with Hal Austin and his associate, Norman Duffett, to talk about election paraphernalia, including large posters. Before joining the Austin Advertising Agency, Duffett had worked for twenty-five years in the advertising department of Ayre & Sons on Water Street, where he established his reputation as one of the most gifted show-card writers and layout men in the business. On the day we met, as Austin and I were talking about the type and quantity of signs I would need, Duffett was busy with a drafting pencil and a pad, sketching a logo and several rough layouts of signs for my campaign, and calculating the cost.

Duffett's logo and suggested sign layout were exactly what I wanted, except for their estimated cost, which would exceed my total campaign budget.

Without giving it a second thought, I asked Austin if he was prepared to gamble on my chances of being elected. If I won the election, I would pay his company double the cost of the signs; if I didn't win, I would pay them nothing. Without a moment's hesitation, Austin and Duffett accepted my proposition. Obviously, they had more confidence in my ability to win than I did.

The longer I thought about it afterwards, the more convinced I became that it was a good deal. As a newcomer to St. John's municipal politics and relatively unknown, I would be up against twelve other candidates, most of whom were prominent, well known people whose family roots were deeply embedded in old St. John's. My family roots were equally embedded, but in Greenspond, an island fishing community on the province's northeast coast, not in St. John's.

The five sitting councillors were also well known, household names in the St. John's area. Defeating any of them would not be easy. The only way I could possibly do it was to mount an aggressive, effective campaign. Since I had less than a month to make myself known and recognizable to the St. John's electorate, I was convinced I would have to depart from the old, conservative methods used by candidates in past municipal elections and try something new and eye-catching. At the appropriate time, I would plaster the entire city with my signs and picture.

With the arrangement I had with Austin Advertising Agency, there was no need for a sign shortage. If I won the election, my income for the four-year term as councillor would more than offset the cost of the campaign; if I didn't win, it wouldn't matter. Because winning the 1961 election was important to my pursuit of a political career, I was prepared to spend my entire four-year salary on the campaign, if that was what it took to win.

My strategy was to have my campaign workers, equipped with ladders and staplers, hit the streets before daylight ten days before election day and literally plaster the city with my signs. Harold Grandy, an old friend of mine who worked with the Department of Education, was my unofficial campaign manager. He and I spent several hours driving around St. John's, identifying prime spots for my 4' x 8' signs. In all but a few cases, the owners of the properties we identified were more than willing to cooperate. Obviously, it was Grandy's superb negotiating skill, not the popularity of the unknown candidate, that accounted for our success.

My plan worked. As the people of St. John's went to work on the morning of November 4, 1961, it was virtually impossible for them not to see one or more of my signs. They were strategically placed on buildings and utility poles, and at intersections in all areas of the city. Within a few hours I was the most talked about candidate running in the election, and as recognizable as the rest of them. In a place where it was unheard of for candidates in a municipal election to erect large signs, the voters of North America's oldest city were entering a new era in municipal politics. Election campaigns in staid, conservative St. John's would never be the same.

There would be other surprises in store for the citizens of St. John's before the 1961 election was over. On the last Saturday of the campaign, they were treated to another first—aerial campaigning. Jim Fagan and I were good friends of Jim Collins, who owned and operated a small aircraft charter service. At the time, Collins was engaged in open warfare with the St. John's City Council over its refusal to permit him to land his float-equipped aircraft on Quidi Vidi Lake. A typical fighting St. John's Irishman, Collins was not about to roll over and play dead. If he could not get what he wanted from the present council, he would put his money where his mouth was and help bring about its demise. At the appropriate time, he would crisscross the skies over St. John's in one of his small planes with an attention-grabbing campaign banner in tow, displaying in large red letters: "Vote for Carter and Fagan." Naturally, neither Fagan nor I did anything to discourage Collins' involvement.

I made the most of the double-or-nothing sign deal I had with Hal Austin. As the aircraft flew our banner over the city, a motorcade of sixty or seventy vehicles, decorated with ribbons and "Carter for Council" signs, and with Irish jigs blaring from a public address system, made its way through the streets of St. John's, including Water Street, the higher levels, and the back of town. Fortunately, the person responsible for the air show that afternoon was better organized than the ones responsible for organizing and planning the motorcade route. The whole exercise was a comedy of errors, a typical example of Murphy's law. Anything that could go wrong went wrong.

Having the motorcade go up Water Street on a busy Saturday afternoon was the most serious blunder of all. Before the advent of suburban shopping malls, Water Street on a fine November weekend was like a circus. It was almost impossible to control the large number of people and automobiles that descended on the downtown area.

Our motorcade entered Water Street from Prescott Street at approximately 2:00 P.M., and what followed was almost too bizarre to describe. Suffice it to say, we disrupted traffic and business in the entire downtown area. Water Street traffic almost ground to a complete halt the moment we arrived, and remained that way for an hour. By the time we were ready to leave Water Street and head up Patrick Street and Hamilton Avenue to LeMarchant Road, we managed to alienate virtually everybody in the downtown area, including the city police, store owners, shoppers, cab and bus drivers and passengers. It took us—and the other traffic caught in the

Motorcade going up Hamilton Avenue during my first Municipal
campaigne in 1961. Note the sign.

motorcade—the best part of an hour to travel through the
downtown shopping area, which is considerably less than a
mile.

There were other equally hilarious treats in store for the
good citizens of St. John's on that fateful afternoon. There
were in the 1961 municipal campaign several issues of great
concern to the St. John's electorate, not the least of which was
the location of the city dump. Home owners in the Empire
Avenue area—called "Little Bonavista" because of the large
number of former Bonavista Bay people who lived
there—had a very serious problem. The municipal garbage
dump was situated on land abutting the north side of Empire
Avenue within a few hundred feet of their homes. It was
making life almost unbearable, not to mention the negative
impact it was having on the resale value of their homes. The
area residents who took pride in their new homes and sur-
roundings were inundated with every pest known to mankind, including rats, flies, seagulls and stray animals. There
were also foul-smelling odours from the hundreds of tons of
household and industrial garbage dumped in the area daily
and left uncovered to decompose.

Almost every home owner in "Little Bonavista" whose

family roots, like mine, were in Bonavista Bay, actively worked on my campaign. They saw in me their only hope for a resolution of their problems with the dump. They contacted their friends and relatives in other parts of the city, sent out personal letters and made hundreds of telephone calls soliciting support for my candidacy. Even though it was assumed that I would fight for the removal of the dump, this was never a condition of their support. However, it should be noted that within a year of the election, work on the relocation of the garbage dump on Empire Avenue to its present location in Robin Hood Bay was underway.

Another issue that plagued candidates in every St. John's municipal council campaign was the rivalry that existed between the east and west ends of the city. People living in the west end were convinced that the east end was receiving preferential treatment from city hall. Conversely, the east end residents were convinced that the city's west end was favoured.

When the route for the motorcade was being planned, I made sure that these two issues were not overlooked. I arranged to have a stake-body truck in the motorcade, in which two of my campaign workers would perform a special function. I had the Austin Advertising Agency make three large plywood signs, which the men in the back of the truck were to hold up for all to see at the appropriate times and places.

As the motorcade entered the west end of St. John's, historically the area west of Carter's Hill, the workers would hold up the sign, "West End Can Count on Carter." Proceeding east of Carter's Hill, they would hold up the sign intended for the city's east end, "East End Can Count on Carter." My instruction concerning the third sign was equally explicit. As the motorcade approached Empire Avenue, the workers were told to hold up the sign, "The Dump Must Go—Vote for Carter."

First meeting of St. John's City Council after the 1961 election. Seated
around the table from left to right: Walter Carter, Geoff Carnell,
William Adams, Sir Brian Dunfield, Mayor Harry Mews, City Clerk
E.B. Foran, James Higgins, Alex Henley and James Fagan.

My plan began to fall apart on Water Street West. As the
motorcade started up Patrick Street, the heart of the city's
west end, I looked around as the truck carrying the signs was
turning the corner of Water and Patrick Streets. To my
horror, I saw the sign on which was painted, "East End Can
Count on Carter."

For reasons which I discovered later, they were incapable
of following my instructions, and the whole exercise back-
fired. The sign that was supposed to be held up only as long
as it took the motorcade to drive through the area where the
municipal dump was located was still being held up as we
entered the heart of the city's east end. In the confusion—and, as I discovered, in their drunken stupor—as we
proceeded east on Military Road, on our way to the stadium
parking lot in the city's extreme east end, they were seen
holding up the sign: "West End Can Count on Carter."

The empty rum bottle found later in the back of the truck
told the whole story. By the time the motorcade was ready to
disperse, the men were so drunk they had to be physically
removed from the truck and driven home.

Fourteen

The Longshoremen and the Sir Humphrey Gilbert Building

In its heyday, the Longshoremen's Protective Union (LSPU) was the most successful union in Newfoundland. Experiencing phenomenal growth in the first decade of its existence, its membership reached 3,400 workers. For more than half a century, stevedoring was one of the largest sources of employment in the St. John's area.

The LSPU was noted for its solidarity and clannishness. The membership usually voted in a block in municipal elections, making it a potent political force in the capital city. Several of its leaders were actively involved in municipal politics, including a young St. John's lawyer, Michael Patrick Gibbs, who at the turn of the century was instrumental in launching the LSPU. Gibbs served as St. John's mayor from 1906 to 1910. Elected to the House of Assembly, he served as President of the Legislative Council until 1934, when Responsible Government was suspended and replaced with the Commission of Government.

Most longshore workers lived downtown, their favourite hangout being Duckworth Street east of the War Memorial, where they had an unobstructed view of St. John's Harbour and the Narrows. In the first half of this century, very few homes in the older parts of St. John's had telephones. Keeping an eye on the harbour for the arrival of ships was the only way the longshoremen had of knowing when to report for work.

In the mid-1950s, overriding the objections of hundreds of longshoremen, the federal government announced its intention to construct a new, seven-story office building on land situated between Duckworth and Water Streets, precisely where longshore workers had been congregating for decades. Intended to be Newfoundland's largest federal government building, it would cover the entire area from the War Memorial east to the corner of Cochrane and Duckworth Streets.

The announcement was well received. It was generally felt that the building would not only inject new life into that part of the downtown, but its construction would also generate considerable short-term benefits for the construction and building supply industry. It was also welcome news for the St. John's City Council which saw it as a new source of tax revenue for the city's coffers. But many of the people who lived in that section of old St. John's, including hundreds of longshoremen, didn't want it. The very thing that motivated them to build and occupy homes there was the view it afforded of the harbour entrance and the entry of the vessels on which they worked. This would be destroyed. Members of the LSPU were up in arms. They circulated petitions and presented them to the city fathers, demanding that council refuse to issue a building permit.

The public showed absolutely no interest in the issue. They were more interested in the economic benefits that would flow from the project than they were in preserving a hangout for longshoremen. Consequently, a building permit was issued, the site was fenced off, and work on the building commenced. Out of force of habit, or perhaps sheer stubbornness, longshoremen continued to congregate in the area after the building was completed, even though their view of the harbour and the Narrows was now completely obstructed.

As if that were not bad enough, shortly after the structure was officially opened and occupied, workers at the Sir Humphrey Gilbert building, as it was named, lodged a complaint with the St. John's City Council that the longshoremen were still congregating in front of their building. According to the office workers, the longshoremen were spending their days "guzzling Pinky and using the most profane language imaginable...a steady stream of four-letter words," they complained. They wanted Council to erect signs on the building prohibiting loitering, especially by longshoremen.

Union spokesmen were quick to respond, "How dare these shaggin' mainlanders accuse us of using bad language? It isn't enough that they block our view of the harbour and interfere with our livelihood. Now they want to banish us from the street altogether."

Entering municipal politics in 1961, I soon discovered that the council was the most exclusive, old-boys club in the city. Membership in the exclusive City Club, where the elite spent their time sipping Scotch on the rocks and playing bridge, was a prerequisite. At thirty-one, I was the youngest person ever elected to Council and the first native-born "Bonavista bayman."

The St. John's City Election Act, under which municipal elections were conducted, was as antiquated as some of the councillors. In a city of approximately 75,000 people, only 11,000 had a vote. Some holders of multiple voting rights represented tremendous voting power. When I first ran for council, J. V. Ryan, who was in charge of the Railway Employees Welfare Association, was entitled to cast a vote for each and every property owned by the Association. For obvious reasons, Jimmy Ryan was wooed and courted by every candidate. I dropped in on him during the campaign and was astonished to see a pile of voting cards on his desk, each worth a vote. I was not sure how many votes he had, but considering the number of residential properties owned by the REWA in the city's west end, especially on Craigmiller Avenue and Old

Topsail Road, it was not difficult to understand why he was so popular with candidates seeking a Council seat.

As a newcomer to municipal politics and relatively unknown, I knew I would have to work harder, knock on more doors and, wherever possible, align myself with influential groups in the City, including the LSPU, if I wanted to win.

With about a week left in the campaign, one evening I received a telephone call from a man whose voice I recognized as that of an old longshoreman friend of mine, Leo Maher. In his heavy St. John's Irish accent, he told me that he and a few of his friends were having a meeting in Jim's Tavern on Water Street, to decide the extent of their involvement in the upcoming municipal election. From the racket in the background, it was obvious that they were also having refreshments. Leo told me that St. John's longshore workers were simply not going to put up with it any longer. "They had no right putting that shaggin' Gilbert building where they put it, and blocking our view of the harbour. We're here tonight talking it over to see what we can do about it."

I have never met a St. John's longshoreman I did not like. They are a rare breed, epitomizing the soul and character of the native-born St. John's townie. In the five elections I fought and won in St. John's, I could not have succeeded without the help and loyal support of the people who live in the older parts of the city, including hundreds of longshoremen and their families. My friend Leo Maher was no exception. There was more human kindness, loyalty and common decency in his little finger than I have seen in most of the political people I have known and served with over the years, including a couple of Premiers. Which is why I was prepared to give Leo and his friends a respectful hearing. Although the nature of his call and the circumstances under which it was made might have been a little out of the ordinary, I was willing to listen to what he had to say.

It was obvious that the patrons of Jim's Tavern supported

the tone and content of Leo's telephone conversation. Whenever he mentioned possible alternatives, including such measures as "blowing the shaggin' thing out of the ground," a cheer would go up in the background, followed by a hearty round of applause. I asked Leo what he and the boys wanted me to do; I was assured they meant business.

"If you support us in our fight to force the federal government to move the Gilbert Building to another site, we will help you get elected to City Council," Leo said. He reminded me that such support from their union practically guaranteed my election.

Trying not to be too flippant, I told my friend that it would not be easy to lift a seven-story, 125,000-square-foot, steel-frame, masonry building, and relocate it to another part of the City.

"Obviously," I said, "I could not make such a promise." Choosing my words carefully, I said, "Leo, listen carefully to what I am going to say. Tell your friends that I will back them to the hilt, if they can convince me that it is possible, from an engineering and cost point of view, to move the Gilbert Building to another site. Convince me that it's possible and I'm with you."

"Fair enough," Leo said."That's as much as we could hope to get from anybody."

Leo repeated on the telephone every word I said for the others to hear. The shouting and applause in the background convinced me that I had said precisely what they wanted to hear, even though both Leo and I knew that it meant nothing. What really mattered was that for the first time since the controversy started, a politician was prepared to listen to what they had to say, even if it did not make sense. They had been completely ignored by the mayor and councillors when they had raised the matter before the building permit was issued.

Obviously, Leo and the boys were in the mood to vent

their spleen and flex their collective political muscle. They knew as well as I did that their fight to retain their favourite hangout on Duckworth Street was lost the moment construction on the Sir Humphrey Gilbert Building commenced. But perhaps they had a good point. There were other, less congested sites in St. John's where the building could have been erected. Meanwhile, had I refused to listen and dismissed the fellows like a bunch of fools, it is quite possible that the outcome of the election, at least for me, would have been quite different.

Fifteen

Bertie, the Loose Cannon

St. John's is not only a city of legends and characters; it is also a city of traditions. One such tradition is the New Year's Day levees: members of the male gentry visit the heads of church and state to pay their respects. As New Year's Day approaches, notices appear in the local newspapers advising the public of the New Year's day levees or "at homes."

Traditionally, the Lieutenant-Governor, the heads of the Roman Catholic, Anglican and United Churches, along with the mayor of St. John's, are at home on New Year's Day to receive well-wishers and exchange New Year's greetings. Usually, the Roman Catholic Archbishop is the first off the mark. Callers start arriving at his official residence at eleven o'clock, to be met in the foyer by a priest and formally presented to His Grace. The others, including the mayor, begin receiving callers at two o'clock in the afternoon.

A philosopher once said that people who want to under-stand democracy should spend less time in the library with Aristotle and more time on the buses and in the subway. The New Year's Day levee in St. John's—in which the formally dressed city elite sometimes have to stand in line with the ordinary folks and wait their turn to be recognized and presented—is an even better example of democracy in ac-tion. Mind you, most of the visitors are the upper crust. Occasionally, though, a few local ne'er-do-wells make their way to the various at-home venues, hoping to cash in on whatever freebies are on the go.

My introduction to the New Year's Day levee circuit was

in 1962, a few hours after being sworn in as a member of the
St. John's City Council. Following a long-established tradition, council members made the rounds of the various levees
to pay their respects. Usually, a city-owned vehicle and driver
chauffeured the city fathers around, starting with a visit to the
Roman Catholic Archbishop.

At that time we were living on Graves Street on the back
of town, and I was the last one to be picked up. Mayor Mews
and the other councillors, all of whom lived in the older
sections of the city, were already in the station wagon when it
arrived for me. Since this was my first official function, I
invited my new colleagues into my home to meet my family
and to take refreshments. I wanted to make a good impression on my colleagues, especially on the mayor who, as a
member of the St. John's establishment and a true-blue
townie, had very little time or respect for anything or anyone
that came out of the bay.

Harry Mews was first elected mayor in 1949. For sixteen
years he presided over the most exclusive old boys' club in St.
John's. During Commission of Government (from 1934 to
1949) members of the St. John's City Council were the only
publicly elected officials in Newfoundland. Then and for a
considerable time following the return of elected government, election to city council carried with it an aura of
prestige and respectability seldom accorded members of
municipal government.

The prerequisites for election to the Council before 1961
were your standing in the Roman Catholic, Anglican or
United Church, your social status, and the extent to which the
business community trusted you. For some inexplicable reason, it did not matter how many candidates were running, or
their religious affiliation; when the votes were counted, the
outcome was predictable. The new council would be com-
prised of three Roman Catholics and three Protestants. More
often than not, the successful candidates were those with the

greatest following within their religious denomination. Invariably, they would be St. John's-born, upper-middle-class members of the various social clubs.

My election to the council was the first time an "out-harbour man" managed to crack the armour of the old boy's club. It was also the first time a person who was not upper-class, a member of an elite social club, or a prominent member of one of the three leading religious denominations, managed to get elected to Council.

I welcomed the opportunity that presented itself on that New Year's morning to show off what I had: a modest, story-and-a-half home which I had built as a participant in a twelve-member Cooperative Housing Group; seven beautiful, healthy children; a young, very attractive wife; and a housekeeper, Bertie. Our eighth child, Susan, was born the following year.

I soon found out that with a loose cannon like Bertie on the premises, inviting my colleagues into my home was a terrible mistake. Bertie was a young woman we had hired to help with the children, all of whom were under eleven years of age. Having grown up in a middle-class environment, Muriel and I had no idea how to manage domestic help. We instinctively treated Bertie like one of the family and went out of our way to make her feel at home. Once Bertie became aware of this, it became a question of who, exactly, was the servant—was Bertie working for us, or were we working for her? She was not content merely to be treated like one of the family—she proceeded to take over.

There were other problems too. Since this was Bertie's first job and her first time away from home, she had no idea about what was expected of her as a domestic worker, or how she should conduct herself in such an environment. Born and raised in a small, northern community, Bertie was a rambunctious eighteen-year-old who was not imbued with the rules of good etiquette or exposed to the teachings of Emily Post or

Amy Vanderbilt. She was a diamond in the rough, whose crude habits and foul language eventually caused her to lose her job.

Bertie was intrigued by the manner in which the mayor and the councillors were dressed. Obviously, this was the first time she had ever seen men in formal morning attire. I tried my best to act as if I were accustomed to wearing morning clothes. However, the moment I entered the living room wearing striped trousers and a swallowtail coat, the expression on Bertie's face confirmed my worst fears: I knew that she was going to make a show of me.

She just stood there with her hands on her hips, looking at me. Shaking her head and trying to control a fit of laughter, she said, "Mr. Carter, where in the name of Christ did ya get that outfit? Youse looks just like a bullbird."

I tried to make light of Bertie's remark, telling her to go out in the kitchen and look after the children. A few minutes later she returned to the living room where we were standing around, sipping a drink. Again she wanted to know where I had gotten the "Gawd-awful, foolish-looking outfit" I was wearing. "I've never seen that around here before. Is it yours?"

My colleagues were thoroughly enjoying Bertie's antics. She was the centre of attraction. Finally, I told Bertie that while it was none of her business, she was quite correct in saying that she had not seen me wearing morning clothes before; this was the first time. "In fact," I said, "this suit does not even belong to me. It was rented for the occasion from a downtown tailor."

Bertie was flabbergasted. "What next!" she exclaimed. "Youse means to say that strangers was wearing them pants before youse put em on?"

Turning to the Mayor who was splitting his sides laughing, she sized him up for a few seconds and then said, "And how 'bout you, skipper. Is them pants youse got on rented,

too?" Before he could answer, she looked around the room at the others and proceeded to deliver a stinging reprimand: "If youse fellers is not careful," she said, gazing about at us as we stood around the living room, "one of these days, youse'll all end up with a dose o' the clap."

Parachute Candidate and Next Premier

Sixteen

Develop or Perish

The wait that usually precedes the calling of a general election in Newfoundland was finally over: Premier Joseph R. Smallwood's governing Liberals had been given an overwhelming majority three years earlier, and on October 18, 1962, he made the customary visit to Government House. One hour later, he emerged to announce that on November 19 the people of Newfoundland and Labrador would be going to the polls to elect a new government—for the fifth time since Confederation.

In a province-wide radio and television address later that evening, Smallwood revealed that he would ask the people of Newfoundland and Labrador for a mandate: authorizing his government to proceed immediately with a $70 million fisheries development program.

Most political observers were not fooled by the events leading up to the election call—in any case, they didn't fool easily. In another province-wide radio and television broadcast two months earlier, Smallwood had fired what was obviously the first shot in the upcoming election campaign: he announced that the government would sponsor a three-day fisheries conference, to be held in St. John's in September.

In typical Smallwood fashion, he issued a call to arms: "I now call upon the fishermen and merchants of Newfoundland to come together in this great convention to make the greatest attempt ever to find a good working plan that will bring prosperity to our fisheries, merchants and fishermen." Categorizing it as "the most important conference of its kind

On the way up the Great Northern Peninsula in November, 1962 on the way to open the new road to kick off the election campaign in White Bay North. In the picture from left to right: Gerald Hill; James R. Chalker; William J. Lundrigan; Premier Smallwood; Dr. Fred Rowe; Max Lane; Walter Carter.

ever held in Newfoundland," he said, "All Newfoundlanders and Labradorians who are concerned about the fisheries will be invited." The political jargon revealed that an election was imminent, and drove the message home to everyone, especially the Opposition.

The leaders of the other parties pretended to have been taken completely by surprise, despite all the earlier signs. Their usual criticism about the hasty election call was accompanied by a prediction of the outcome: they were all going to win a majority government. In fact, to accommodate the total number of seats the three parties were predicting to win, an additional 58 seats would have to be added to the 42-seat Legislature. We would end up with a 100-seat Legislature—far too large and unwieldy for a province this size.

The guessing game—who would and would not be running—got off to a good start, and opinions were abundant and colourful. Word had it that Smallwood was going to raid municipal councils around the Island for candidates. There was speculation that he would be running popular St. John's Deputy Mayor Bill Adams in the District of St. John's West, and equally popular Councillor Jim Higgins in St. John's East. He would recruit Councillor James Fagan for St. John's East Extern and Geoff Carnell for St. John's North. Even I was not exempt from the wild and often unfounded speculation: because of my "out harbour" upbringing, the St. John's wags had me running in one of the northern districts.

The greatest stir was caused by the speculation that Jim Higgins would be running for the Liberal Party in the old family stomping grounds of St. John's East. The St. John's Tory establishment was stunned—they could not understand what "Jimmy" was up to. What had Smallwood offered him? Was he promised a Cabinet post or perhaps a Supreme Court judgeship? Speculation flew fast and furious. They were prepared to overlook Higgins' split with the federal Tories in 1959—the result of a dispute that arose between Smallwood and Prime Minister John Diefenbaker over Diefenbaker's interpretation of Term 29 of the Terms of Union between Newfoundland and Canada. They would even overlook what happened that same year when Higgins and two of his Tory colleagues, St. John's businessmen Gus Duffy and John R. O'Dea, bolted the Party and formed the United Newfoundland Party which subsequently contested the 1959 general election. "But surely," they said among themselves, "our Jimmy wouldn't sink so low as to run for the Smallwood Liberals!"

The Higgins name, a household word in the east end of St. John's, had been always synonymous with the Progressive Conservative Party. It had started back in the 1913 general election, when the patriarch of the Higgins clan, William J. ("Billy") Higgins, caused a major upset. He was one of the three members elected in St. John's East for Sir Edward P. Morris' People's Party, ending the Liberal Party's three-decade monopoly in the District. The senior Higgins remained active in Newfoundland politics until 1928, when he was appointed to the Bench of the Newfoundland Supreme Court.

The next Higgins to arrive on the political scene in St. John's East was Gordon F. Higgins, Jim's brother. After being governed since 1934 by Commission of Government, Newfoundlanders were told by Prime Minister Clement Attlee on December 11, 1945 that the British government would make it possible for them to decide their constitutional future. A general election would be held in 1946 to select delegates for a national convention which would examine our country's position and recommend possible forms of future government. Probable scenarios would then be put before the people of Newfoundland in a referendum.

For the first time in twelve years, Newfoundlanders and Labradorians went to the polls to elect 45 delegates to the National Convention. Gordon Higgins ran in St. John's East and was one of the three members elected to represent St. John's.

Shortly after the National Convention was called, Smallwood, establishing himself firmly as the Confederate leader, introduced a motion proposing that a delegation be sent to Ottawa to discuss the possibility of Newfoundland's union with Canada. Although he was adamantly opposed to Confederation, Gordon Higgins seconded Smallwood's motion and was subsequently appointed to the Ottawa delegation.

When, after two referenda and considerable acrimonious debate, Newfoundland became a Canadian province, it was allotted seven seats in the Canadian House of Commons. Gordon Higgins' candidacy in the federal riding of St. John's East for the Tory Party came as no surprise. His strong opposition to Confederation and his ongoing association with the St. John's anti-Confederate establishment (most of whom sought refuge in the Tory Party after the 1948 referendum) guaranteed his election.

Another prominent member of the Higgins family involved in Newfoundland politics was John Gilbert Higgins, an uncle of Jim and Gordon. He too was an ardent anti-confederate who successfully contested St. John's East as a Progressive Conservative in the first provincial general election after Confederation. With the electoral defeat of Tory leader H.G.R. Mews in St. John's West, John Higgins became the first leader of the Progressive Conservative Party to sit in the House of Assembly after Confederation. Until his death on July 2, 1963 in Ottawa, where he was serving as Newfoundland's first Tory Senator, John Higgins remained loyal to the Tory Party, and to the pre-Confederation, Responsible Government movement.

All of this history came into play when tongues wagged over Jim Higgins' possible Liberal candidacy.

Smallwood used to call Jim Higgins "Newfoundland's greatest joiner." There was hardly an organization in St.

John's in which Higgins did not serve. The list includes the St. John's Regatta Committee, the St. John's Football League, the Amateur Athletic Association of Canada, the Newfoundland Federation of Mayors, the Community Planning Association of Canada and, of course, the St. John's City Council. As a prominent Roman Catholic, Higgins served on almost every church and school committee in the diocese. In every sense of the word, Jim Higgins was a star candidate for the Liberal Party in St. John's East.

It soon became obvious to Smallwood watchers that his search for star candidates with municipal experience would not be confined to St. John's City Hall. Scarcely a mayor in rural Newfoundland escaped Smallwood's notice. Lewisporte mayor Harold Starkes, Carbonear mayor Bill Saunders, Bay Roberts mayor Eric Dawe, and Port aux Basques mayor Walter Holder all ended up on the Liberal ticket in the 1962 election. It was reported in the press that other individuals were called but resisted the temptation to become part of the Smallwood team, at least for the time being.

This was not the first time that Smallwood targeted the leaders of select groups and organizations around the province as potential Liberal candidates. It was no secret that Newfoundland's self-styled democrat had no time for the selection of candidates through the nomination process. He jealously guarded his self-proclaimed right to select the people whose names would appear on his ticket and who would sit behind him in the House of Assembly following the election.

It should be noted that targeting municipal councils as a source of star candidates was not confined to the Liberal Party in that election. The Progressive Conservative Party was doing the same thing.

And, although I did not carry the cachet of Jim Higgins, I was for the first time in the position to be approached.

Seventeen

Smallwood Calling

It started off for the Carter family like any other day: the usual confusion at breakfast time, the rush to get the children off to school and Muriel's last-minute admonitions, "Be sure to listen to the teacher. Don't forget your recess money. Come straight home after school."

At the time, I owned and operated a real estate and house-building business in St. John's, and was also a member of the St. John's City Council. After driving our children to school, I went to my office to attend a meeting of my sales staff and prepare myself for a ten o'clock meeting at City Hall.

As I was preparing to leave, my secretary said, "Premier Smallwood's secretary wants to speak to you on the telephone." In her usual stern and authoritative voice, Muriel Templeman told me the Premier wanted to meet me in the lobby of Confederation Building at two o'clock that afternoon. "Try to be there on time," she said. I knew better than to ask her what the Premier wanted. Muriel Templeman was from the old school; she knew her place, and she was a person of few words. If she thought I should know in advance what the Premier wanted me for, she would have told me. I knew there was no point in asking her.

Muriel Templeman went to work for Smallwood in the old Confederate office on Water Street in 1947, soon after he launched the campaign for Confederation. She probably knew more about Smallwood's personal life, his moods and idiosyncrasies than any other person alive. The first thing Smallwood did after he was sworn in as Premier of Canada's newest province was to hire Muriel Templeman as his special assistant. He gave her a free hand to run his office. And run it she did—with an iron fist. It did not matter who or what you were; if you wanted access to the Premier, you quickly discovered that it would not be in your best interest to get in Muriel Templeman's bad books. It was widely believed that she wielded more influence on Smallwood than all his ministers together. She knew the time-wasters and the hangers-on, and when it was necessary she knew how to get rid of them. She protected Smallwood like a mother hen.

I arrived in the lobby of Confederation Building as the Premier was leaving the elevator. Without saying a word, he headed towards me, shook my hand, took me by the arm, and led me to his black Cadillac sedan, parked in front of the building. Dressed in his usual dark, ultra-conservative black overcoat, matching black suit and black homburg, he looked more like a Jesuit priest than a politician. Coincidentally or otherwise, most of his ministers also wore dark clothing, especially when they were accompanying "the Skipper" on official business.

The afternoon of October 28, 1962 was no exception. As Smallwood was hustling me down the steps of Confederation Building, three men, dressed in black and wearing black homburgs, were sitting in the car waiting for us. The entire setting reminded me of a scene from the television series "The Untouchables." The only thing missing was the machine gun.

Approaching the car, I immediately recognized its occupants. In the front seat sat Smallwood's long-time heir presumptive, Dr. Fred Rowe, who was then the Minister of Highways. Sitting in the rear seat was the Attorney General, Leslie Curtis, puffing on an oversized cigar. Next to Curtis sat city councillor Geoffrey Carnell who was also dressed in black, but for another reason. Carnell was the city's leading funeral director and had just returned from a funeral; he was still wearing striped trousers and a black swallowtail coat, or as he used to call it, his working clothes. To my dismay, I found myself sitting in the back seat, sandwiched between Carnell and Curtis who, between them, weighed well over a quarter ton if they weighed an ounce.

Joey Smallwood had a reputation for being a reckless driver. He was often seen driving at excessive speeds over Seal Cove Barrens, sometimes with a sheep or some other farm animal in the back seat, headed for his farm on Roaches Line. Earlier that week, a regular caller to an open line radio show had reported that she had seen Joey that morning speeding over the Conception Bay Highway with a full-grown ram sprawled out on the back seat of his Cadillac.* "The poor thing looked exhausted," the caller said. "I suppose the long trip across the Atlantic and, on top of that, not knowing what was expected of him on Roaches Line."

There were many stories making the rounds during that time about the imported ram. Since members of the Opposition had started a rumour that the government had borne the cost of purchasing and transporting the ram to the province, the animal was frequently referred to as "the government ram." A few days later another caller to the same open line program said that she too had seen Smallwood driving in his Cadillac over Seal Cove Barrens, with the government ram sprawled out in the back seat. A later caller insisted that the previous caller must have been mistaken, for she could not possibly have seen Joey with the government ram in his car on the day in question.

Asked by the program's moderator how she could be so sure, she replied, "My Gawd, Ron, I s'pose I'd know if it was

---

* The ram she saw in Smallwood's Cadillac had arrived in St. John's the previous day from Scotland. During a visit to the U.K. Smallwood bought it for breeding purposes on his ranch on Roaches Line.

the Attorney General in the car with Joey. Not only that, 'tis on the news this morning that he's over in Switzerland or somewhere, gallivanting around as usual." She was referring to Leslie Curtis, who had a reputation for being less than discreet when it came to his involvement with members of the fairer sex.

The drive to St. Phillips was nerve-wrecking. As we left the parking lot in front of Confederation Building and entered Prince Philip Drive, it became obvious that Smallwood was no respecter of restricted speed zones. Not content to drive 60 miles an hour in a 30-mile zone, he suddenly decided to plug in his portable electric razor and shave himself.

Smallwood was of small physical stature. When he sat behind the wheel of his oversized Cadillac, the only thing visible to people in the back seat was a black homburg and a hand on the steering wheel. As we took the 90-degree turn at the entrance to Thorburn Road, I saw the black homburg turn towards Dr. Rowe. Shouting to be heard over the buzz of the electric razor, Smallwood said, "Fred, if you were a young fellow about Walter Carter's age and had ambitions to get into politics, which district would you go after? Would you go for a St. John's seat, or would you go after an outport seat?"

Trying to act nonchalant, Rowe replied, "My goodness, Mr. Premier, it goes without saying that I would go after a safe outport seat—some place like White Bay North."

After a short pause, the questioning continued, "Fred, if you were an Anglican—Walter, you are an Anglican, aren't you? Okay, Fred, if you were an Anglican like Walter, which district would you choose if you wanted to have a long and successful career in politics?"

Rowe replied, "Again, Mr. Premier, the answer is obvious. It would have to be White Bay North."

Showing a total lack of concern about oncoming traffic and still travelling enormously fast, Smallwood swung his head around and said to his Attorney General in the back,

"Les, if you were a young man—Walter Carter's age—just starting out in politics and had what it takes to be Premier, if you had a choice, where would you run?"

Still puffing on his oversized cigar, and finding it difficult to keep a straight face, the veteran campaigner, who kept the Twillingate voters tightly in his grip for a dozen years, knew what he was expected to say. "There's no doubt about it, Joe," he answered. "My first choice would be White Bay North." As if suddenly remembering on which side his bread was buttered, Curtis quickly added, "On second thought, Joe, it would be a toss-up between White Bay North and Twillingate."

Geoff Carnell, the other half of the human vice that held me in its grip in the back seat of the car, was getting a kick out of Smallwood's shenanigans. Earlier that day, Carnell had committed himself to run for the Liberals in St. John's North, a seat about to be vacated by former St. John's councillor George Nightingale, who was retiring from provincial politics. Carnell's candidacy would be announced the following day along with several others. Carnell kept jabbing me in the ribs and whispering under his breath, "Hang in there, buddy. Uncle Joe is getting ready to pop the question."

We were scheduled to make a short stop at the Sunshine Camp, a facility for children with disabilities operated by the St. John's Rotary Club, and located about halfway between St. John's and St. Phillips. Approaching the camp, we saw several nurses and other staff members congregated on the side of the road with a group of children who were cheering and waving little flags. They wanted to see Joey and shake his hand. Smallwood slowed down to give the media people, who were following in another car, time to catch up and shoot television footage of what was about to occur. When he was satisfied they were ready, he pulled off to the side of the road and emerged from his car like a conquering hero amid the spontaneous cheers of adults and children alike. What a great way to kick off an election campaign! I thought. Smallwood shook every hand in the crowd, spoke to the children, signed autographs, and praised the nurses and other staff members for their dedication and hard work. He thanked the Rotary Club for their generosity and the exemplary manner in which they were operating the Sunshine Camp.

He then paid a special tribute to a past president of Rotary, Geoffrey C. Carnell who, he said, helped make it all possible. "Geoffrey Carnell is not only an outstanding Rotarian," he said. "He is also an outstanding Newfoundlander." He predicted that they would be hearing much more about Councillor Carnell in the days ahead. With that, we climbed back into the car, on our way to take part in yet another political milestone. Smallwood would cut a ribbon and tamp down the last shovelful of asphalt, officially marking the completion of the road to St. Phillips.

Smallwood was in his glee. He kept his foot on the accelerator until the car had again reached an excessive speed. At that moment he ceremoniously made the announcement we had been waiting for all afternoon.

"Walter," he said, "one day you will be Premier of Newfoundland. But in order for you to become Premier, you must first be elected to the House of Assembly. And to get elected to the House of Assembly, and keep getting re-elected, and re-elected, not once, not twice, but perhaps a half dozen times in your lifetime, you will need a district. Earlier this afternoon you heard me ask Fred and Les what district they would choose to run in if they were in your shoes. You heard their answers. They both agreed that it would not be St. John's North, not Trinity North, not Bonavista North, but White Bay North." Following a long pause, he said, "I am now offering you the opportunity to run in White Bay North."

After going through the motions of pretending to be taken completely by surprise, my first reaction was to ask what would happen to the incumbent, Max Lane. "Is he retiring from politics?" I asked. Lane was one of the people Smallwood recruited from the magistracy in the mid-fifties to enter provincial politics. He successfully contested the election in White Bay North in 1956, and was subsequently appointed to the Smallwood Cabinet as Minister of Fisheries.

During the Second World War, Lane was a magistrate in Greenspond, where he and my family became very close friends. Before agreeing to anything, I would have to be satisfied that my candidacy in White Bay North would not be at the expense of my old friend. If that were to happen, my family would never forgive me.

Smallwood assured me that Max Lane would be taken care of. "In fact," he said, "Max volunteered to step aside in White Bay North to enable you to run there. He'll be running in St. Barbe South, where he will have absolutely no trouble getting elected."

I told Smallwood I would have to discuss the matter with my wife, Muriel, and other members of my family before I could give him my answer. Obviously that annoyed him. Smallwood was not used to being kept waiting for an answer. More often than not, the shoe was on the other foot. Usually, the moment an election was called, there would be a line-up outside his office door of would-be candidates who would give their right arm to be in my place that afternoon.

After another long pause, Smallwood said, "I will give Muriel a call after supper if you think it will help. I must have your answer by eight o'clock tonight, because over the weekend I intend to announce that St. John's Deputy Mayor Bill Adams and councillors Geoff Carnell, Jimmy Higgins and Jim Fagan will be running for the Liberal Party in the election. I would like to be able to announce your candidacy at the same time."

Obviously, he wanted to get as much political mileage as possible from announcing that five of the six men who were elected less than a year earlier to run the affairs of Tory St. John's would be candidates for the Liberal Party in the upcoming election. I assured the Premier that I would not keep him waiting, "You will have my answer by eight o'clock this evening."

As Smallwood was winding up the ribbon-cutting ceremony in St. Phillips, he announced the retirement of George Nightingale, who was first elected to represent St. John's North in the House of Assembly in 1956. Smallwood was loud in his praise of Nightingale, who had immigrated to Newfoundland in 1911 from Liverpool, England. Smallwood listed Nightingale's accomplishments: a St. John's city councillor, a prominent Rotarian, a successful businessman and, of course, the Member for St. John's North. He thanked him for his contribution to the city and to the province. He assured the people of St. John's North that Nightingale's successor would be announced soon.

He then turned his attention to the man he would like to see succeed Nightingale as the Member of the House of Assembly for St. John's North, well known St. John's undertaker and member of city Council, Geoffrey Carnell. He said, "I am working on Councillor Carnell in that regard, and will be having more to say on the subject over the weekend."

For those present, it was an emotional event. George Nightingale was not only a good MHA; to many of his constituents he was also a good friend. During his brief farewell speech or, as he called it, "my swan song," he still showed concern for his constituents. Sensing their discomfort, he tried to make light of his retirement by interjecting a touch of humour. "You must not feel sorry for me," he said. "Things could be a lot worse. My good friend Geoff Carnell could be going ahead of me instead of coming behind me!"

It was a common sight in St. John's in those days, when horse-drawn carriages were used in funeral processions, to see Geoff Carnell walking in front of the casket, attired in a black top hat, striped trousers and a swallowtail coat.

When the significance of Nightingale's remark sank in, he received a tumultuous round of applause.

All of us were in a relaxed, silly mood as we headed back to Confederation Building. Les Curtis set the tone by wondering aloud how many times Billy Higgins would roll over in his grave when he heard the news that his son Jimmy was running for the Liberals in St. John's East, of all places. Smallwood said he was not sure what Billy Higgins would do, but he had a very good idea what Malcolm Hollett and Billy Browne would do. Hollett and Browne were long-time Tories and anti-Confederates. Both represented Tory seats in St. John's and were seeking re-election.

Big, affable Geoff Carnell could not stop laughing. "Yes siree, Uncle Joe," he said. "You've outfoxed all of them this time. I wouldn't want to be the poor old laundryman who'll be washing their shorts. I dare say Boxer Mews and Donkey Furlong won't be needing any castor oil for a while, either." Carnell was referring to Harry Mews, the first leader of the Newfoundland Tory Party after Confederation and St. John's Mayor for sixteen years, and Robert S. Furlong, who was appointed Newfoundland's Chief Justice by the Diefenbaker Tories in 1959. Both were ardent anti-Confederates and had played a prominent role in the Responsible Government League.

I arrived home that evening just in time to watch the evening news on television. The events of the afternoon, including our brief stopover at the Sunshine Camp and the ribbon-cutting ceremony at St. Phillips, were the lead story. My presence at both events with Smallwood did not go unnoticed. It was speculated that Smallwood would be announcing within a few hours my candidacy and that of four other St. John's councillors.

Our children were squatting on the floor around the television set, putting their own spin on what they had just heard. Muriel was sitting back, quietly taking it all in. I asked her what she thought of the idea of my running in White Bay North as a Liberal candidate. Obviously, she had already given it some thought because she did not keep me waiting for an answer. "If that is what you want to do and if it will make you happy, it's fine with me," she said.

We spent the next hour or so sitting around the kitchen table, discussing the pros and cons of my entry into provincial politics. The fact that I was already a member of the St. John's municipal council and owned and operated a fast-growing business had to be taken into consideration. Given the fact that St. John's was predominantly Tory, to what extent would my involvement in the Liberal Party affect my business and my municipal political career? After considering all the odds, we finally made the decision. A couple of minutes before eight o'clock I telephoned Smallwood at his office in Canada House and told him to count me in. "I will be honoured to be your candidate in the district of White Bay North in the upcoming election."

Had we known then the impact my decision would have on my business, my answer would undoubtedly have been different. Four years later, my once-thriving business was on the verge of bankruptcy. Not because of my involvement with the Liberal Party, but because of the extent to which being a city councillor and the Member of the House of Assembly for White Bay North cut into my time. My whole life was taken up with politics, with very little time left for anything else, including my business.

The Premier's confirmation over the weekend that Deputy Mayor Bill Adams and councillors Higgins, Carnell, Fagan and Carter would be Liberal candidates in the November 19 general election drew mixed reaction from the St. John's news media. Most of its members were already less than sympathetic to Smallwood and the Liberal cause. Smallwood's long-standing contempt for the St. John's Tory establishment still smoldered. It did not take much, especially in the excitement of an election campaign, to cause it to erupt. Not content to simply announce our candidacies and leave it at that, Smallwood could not resist the urge to rub salt in the wounds of his old political enemies.

Angered by Smallwood's predictions that they would be wiped out in St. John's, their long-time stronghold, the Tories were furious. They tried to work up the people of St. John's by reminding them that with three years of our term remaining to be served, five of the people whom they elected the previous year to run the city, "have now turned their backs on you and have sold out to Smallwood and the Liberal Party."

Except for a few letters that appeared in the two daily papers, and the usual planted calls to the media newsrooms, the Tory campaign to discredit us in St. John's did not get off the ground. Adams and Carnell won their St. John's seats handily. Higgins and Fagan came within a few hundred votes of winning two of the most Conservative seats in the province, St. John's East and St. John's East Extern. I won White Bay North with the biggest majority in the entire province.

My election to the House of Assembly as a Liberal in an outport district caused me no problem in the subsequent municipal election. While still sitting in the House of Assembly as the MHA for White Bay North, I was re-elected to the St. John's City Council in the 1965 election with a huge majority. I was subsequently named Deputy Mayor to replace John Crosbie who, in 1966, resigned to run for the Liberal Party in the provincial district of St. John's West.

Eighteen

The Next Premier

My initiation into the world of big-time politics in 1962 was not exactly what I had expected. After taking care of the preliminaries, such as taking pictures, ordering posters, and familiarizing myself with the Party's election manifesto, the day arrived for me to leave for White Bay North to start my campaign.

The back-room strategists at Liberal Headquarters thought it would be good politics to kick off the campaign in Northern Newfoundland and Labrador South with the official opening of the partially completed highway up the Great Northern Peninsula from Deer Lake to St. Anthony. It was agreed that the official party would consist of Premier Smallwood, the Minister of Highways, Dr. Fred Rowe, the press, and the Liberal candidates whose districts were served by the new highway, including St. Barbe South and North, White Bay North, and Labrador South.

We would fly to Deer Lake, then travel by car up the Peninsula to St. Anthony, with several campaign stops along the way. The planners estimated the trip would take two full days to complete. What better way to kick off a political campaign! I thought. We'll be taking part in an event that will end centuries of isolation for the 20,000 souls who inhabit the Great Northern Peninsula, including White Bay North.

While under no illusion that we would be flown to Deer Lake in an executive jet, I did have some qualms about having to crawl into the crowded, unheated, uninsulated belly of an antiquated Canso water bomber to start the first leg of my journey into the world of big-time Newfoundland politics. The seating arrangements in the plane also left much to be desired. Makeshift bench-like seats were attached to the sides of the plane's interior, and we were strapped in like paratroopers on their way to a commando raid. The only things missing were parachutes, battle fatigues and machine guns.

Except for being cramped, half frozen to death, and almost shaken out of our skins, it wasn't too bad once the pilot got the plane off the ground and above the clouds. Like any good general leading his troops into battle, Smallwood remained calm and showed no signs of discomfort or nervousness. Seated on a bench just behind the cockpit and using a battery-operated bull horn to be heard over the deafening noise of the engines, he entertained us with a repertoire of the funniest Newfoundland stories I have ever heard. Most of his stories had a political flavour and were related to people known to most of us either in person or by reputation.

Included in the party was a young photographer who had been sent to Newfoundland by his Toronto newspaper to obtain some action shots of Smallwood as he kicked off the campaign. He arrived at the hangar at Torbay Airport with Smallwood, who went out of his way to provide the right setting for a series of unusual pictures. Smallwood introduced the mainland photographer to the rest of the party as we stood around waiting to board the aircraft as "one of Canada's most outstanding photographers, second only to Karsh." Smallwood jokingly cautioned the rest of us to avoid doing anything that we would not want to see on the front page of the *Globe and Mail*. "If you get the urge to pick your nose or scratch your behind, make sure you are out of range of the camera," he cautioned.

The photographer had a field day. He took pictures of Smallwood as he walked towards the aircraft, followed by the rest of us; crawling up through the hatch in the belly of the water bomber; sitting in the pilot's seat and in almost every conceivable position. Smallwood was not shy when it came to availing himself of photo opportunities, especially for the national press.

When the time came for the photographer to board the aircraft, he seemed to hesitate as if he were having second thoughts about going. Finally, he dragged himself up through the hatch and made his way to the bench where the rest of us were seated. From the moment the photographer boarded the aircraft, he seemed extremely nervous, almost on the verge of panic. With his camera hanging loosely over his shoulder, he appeared to have an unusually strong attachment to a thermos bottle he was carrying. He immediately poured himself a cup of its contents, which we assumed was black coffee, and literally poured it down his throat.

Much to the relief of those seated near him, it seemed the more "coffee" he drank, the more he relaxed. After his second cup, we witnessed a remarkable metamorphosis, somewhat like the emergence of a lowly tadpole into a full-grown frog—or, as his media colleagues would have put it by the time we reached our destination, from a maggot to an adult housefly. Our upper-Canadian friend was now thoroughly relaxed and enjoying himself.

The people sitting close to the photographer, including a Cabinet Minister who had a reputation for elbow-bending, were not fooled. Convinced that it contained something stronger than coffee, they kept eyeing the thermos, drooling for a swig of its contents. Unlike Newfoundlanders, who in similar circumstances would be happy to share what they had with a fellow traveller, our mainland photographer friend was obviously not yet imbued with such generosity and good fellowship. He showed absolutely no inclination to share the contents of his thermos with anyone.

Protruding from the roof of the plane's fuselage a couple of feet behind the cockpit was a plexiglass bubble, capable of accommodating an average-size person. It had probably been used as a gun or observation turret by its former wartime occupants. Access to the turret was through a hatch barely large enough to crawl through.

Clutching his thermos as if his life depended on it and with his camera still hanging from his shoulder, the photographer decided he wanted to be alone to sip his "coffee" in peace and perhaps get a new perspective on the universe. By this time, he was showing no signs of nervousness. He staggered towards the front of the plane and dragged himself up through the opening in the roof into the turret. With his legs dangling beneath him and his thermos clutched to his chest, he soon settled away with nothing between him and his Creator but a thin, plexiglass bubble.

As we approached Deer Lake airport, the copilot insisted that, for his own safety, the adventurous photographer would have to return to his bench in preparation for landing. Smallwood, who was seated facing us on a bench attached to the bulkhead behind the copilot, immediately took command of the situation. Trying his best to be patient with the photographer, Smallwood gently tugged on his legs and suggested that he return to his seat and prepare for landing. Receiving no response, he again tried to talk the mainlander into coming down, but without causing him too much fuss or embarrassment. Suddenly, Smallwood grabbed the bull horn and, aiming it directly at the plexiglass turret, shouted to its lone occupant, "Come down from there! Do you hear me? Come down from there immediately!" When he again got no response, he pushed the bull horn closer to the turret and again shouted, "Can you hear me? Are you able to move?"

By this time, Smallwood was visibly angry and in no mood to coddle anybody, not even a mainland photographer. He grabbed the photographer's legs and started to pull. The only thing that came down from the turret was the photographer's camera; it fell to the floor with a thud and came apart. Smallwood looked devastated. The group picture the photographer had taken with such professionalism and his shots of Smallwood posing in the pilot's seat giving a thumbs-up salute were ruined. A few seconds later, an empty thermos, with the cork and cap missing, also flew from the turret and fell to the floor with a loud bang.

Being a non-drinker, Smallwood had very little tolerance for drunks. And, judging by the look on his face, he had absolutely no tolerance for a drunken photographer who showed such disregard for campaign photos, especially those destined for Canada's national newspaper.

The empty, abandoned thermos told the story. We knew then that we were faced with the almost impossible task of extricating an overweight, drunken photographer through a hatch barely large enough to crawl through at the best of times.

Still smarting from the photographer's refusal to share the contents of his thermos, especially under such trying circumstances, his media colleagues appeared not to care if he ever came down. One of them shouted, "Leave the miserable bastard alone, Skipper. He'll pop out of there like a cork out of a bottle the moment this thing hits the runway!"

Arriving in Deer Lake, we were met by members of the Lundrigan family, who arranged to have several cars standing by to take us up the St. Barbe Coast to St. Anthony. The lead car was occupied by the Premier and the candidate whose district we were passing through at the time. Max Lane, whose new district of St. Barbe South commenced a short distance north of Deer Lake, was the first candidate to drive with the Premier in the lead car. When we left St. Barbe South the next day and reached the boundary of St. Barbe North, Lane changed places with Jim Chalker, the candidate for that district.

The first night on the campaign trail was spent in Portland Creek in St. Barbe South. In groups of three, we were assigned cabins owned and operated by the Caines family.

Gerry Hill, the candidate for Labrador South, Chesley Pittman and I were billeted in a cabin with two small bunk rooms and a pullout sofa in the living room. Pittman was a businessman from Great Harbour Deep and a staunch Liberal supporter. He joined us quite by accident in Deer Lake, where he was waiting for transportation to Roddickton to catch a boat to Great Harbour Deep. Everybody on the Great Northern Peninsula knew and respected Ches Pittman. He was one of those Newfoundland outport general merchants who made it possible for people to live in the more isolated communities. He provided the fishermen with fishing gear, gave them whatever they needed to look after their families until the fishing season was over, then bought their fish. He and I became very good friends and remained so until his death in 1994.

When we arrived in the cabin, there was a roaring fire in the woodstove, and on the table we found food and more than enough refreshments, including soft drinks and other treats. We agreed that we had the makings of a good evening. However, before we could settle down in front of the blazing fire and relax, there were more important things to do. We were expected to take our places on stage that night at a rally planned for Max Lane. Since Max had given up his safe White Bay North seat for me, I considered it a privilege to be able to attend his first campaign meeting in his new district and give him whatever moral support I could.

After the introductions and other preliminaries, Smallwood got down to business. He outlined in great detail his eleven-point, $70-million fisheries development program which, he said, was the reason for the election. He wanted a mandate from the people of Newfoundland to initiate a comprehensive fisheries development program.

"It is the biggest job left for me to tackle and conquer while I hold my present position as Premier of Newfoundland," he told a somewhat boisterous audience. "And that,"

he added, "leads me to another question. I have been Premier of this province for more than thirteen years. On top of
that, I had four years of hard work preparing to lead Newfoundland into Confederation with Canada in 1949. I feel
fine now, but I hope and pray I will not have to lead the
government in another election. And that raises the question
of who will succeed me as Premier when I step aside? There
are any number of people highly qualified to take over from
me as leader of the great Liberal Party, and Premier of this
province. In fact, there are a number of men here on this
platform tonight, chafing at the bit to fill my shoes. I have no
doubt that any one of them would make a great Premier."

Pausing for effect, he said, "However, my friends, there is
one man in this hall tonight who stands out from all the rest.
A man who has the experience, compassion, and the stamina
to tackle the job, as well as the determination to get it done."
With that, he swung around and, pointing his finger at Lane,
said, "That man is none other than your candidate, the next
member of the House of Assembly for this district, the man
who will succeed me as Premier of Newfoundland, my good
friend and colleague, Max Lane."

The reaction from the audience left little doubt that there
were many in the hall that night who, as Lane found out after
the votes were counted on November 19, did not share
Smallwood's enthusiasm for candidate Lane. St. Barbe South,
a new district, had within its boundaries a large number of
loggers who were still smarting over Smallwood's ousting of
the International Woodworkers of America union in 1959.
The fact that Max Lane was handpicked by Smallwood to
head the government-sponsored union that replaced the
IWA. in Newfoundland, did not help his cause. The loggers
were still taunted by the words of the ditty that became
synonymous with the Smallwood-Lane campaign to oust
their union and its leader, H. Landon Ladd, "Pick up your
axe and follow Max, and chop off Landon's lad."

Max Lane found out to his dismay that the ghost of H. Landon Ladd still haunted him and Smallwood on the province's west coast. When the votes were counted in the 1962 general election, he lost out to Tory Bill Smith, a Corner Brook lawyer.

As we entered St. Barbe North, the district candidate, Jim Chalker, was given star billing. It was his turn to share the limelight with Smallwood in the lead car, away from the negative influence of the IWA. In every community along the way, children lined up on both sides of the road and waved flags, men fired off muskets and the crowds cheered as we drove by.

Stopping in each community, Smallwood would get out of the car, mingle with the crowd and shake hands. He paid special attention to the children, many of whom had been standing on the sides of the road for hours. When he was satisfied that the crowd was ready, he would grab the loudspeaker, stand on a box or whatever was available to elevate him above the crowd, and make a rousing speech.

That evening we attended a rally in the community hall in Flowers Cove where the district candidate, James Chalker, received most of Smallwood's attention. Unlike the hostility we had encountered the night before in Portland Creek, the meeting in Flowers Cove was a politician's dream come true. The community hall was packed with enthusiastic, solid supporters.

Essentially, the introduction and content of Smallwood's speech were a repeat of the previous evening in Portland Creek. Since most of the people who attended the rally in Flowers Cove were fishermen, there was considerably more enthusiasm for Smallwood's proposed fisheries development plan than there was the previous evening in St. Barbe South, where loggers, still loyal to the IWA, were in the majority. Other than that, the only difference was the name of the person who would succeed Smallwood as Premier; this time it was none other than James R. Chalker.

The drive from Flowers Cove to St. Anthony, where an evening rally in the school auditorium was being planned, was most enjoyable. Within a couple of hours, I thought, we will be in my district, White Bay North, and then it will be my turn. I could hardly wait to be introduced to my future constituents as the next Premier of our province. Surely, I thought, at 32 I would be the youngest Premier in the history of Newfoundland, perhaps in all of Canada.

I could hardly wait for Muriel and our children to hear the news.

Sitting on the stage of the crowded auditorium of the St. Anthony high school while Premier Smallwood introduced me as the Liberal candidate for the district of White Bay North, I could not recognize a single face in the crowd. To make matters worse, not only were the people at the rally strangers, but at that time I didn't know a person in the entire district. In fact, this was my first visit to the Great Northern Peninsula. In every sense of the word, I was a parachute candidate.

The Premier's introduction of me and his glowing description of my accomplishments more than compensated for my lack of familiarity with the area and its people. He referred to me as "an outstanding Bonavista bayman who went to St. John's as a young man and literally took the capital city by storm. This son of a Bonavista Bay fisherman," he shouted, "not only showed the St. John's corner boys how to build good houses, but he also showed them how to run their city."

Smallwood then described how I was elected to city council a year earlier. "He took on all comers," he said, "and whipped the socks off some of the most popular men and women in St. John's who would have given their eyeteeth to win a seat on the St. John's City Council." And, for the third time in as many days, he predicted that the candidate he was introducing would one day be Premier of Newfoundland.

Even though I heard Smallwood make the same prediction several times in recent days about the other candidates, I have to admit it made me feel good. As I sat there and listened, my head was not only spinning, it was swelling.

The following morning, Smallwood and I had breakfast together. He handed me $1,500 to cover my campaign expenses and gave me a few last-minute instructions. He cautioned me against being seen "guzzling beer or hard liquor" on the American Military Base located on the hill overlooking the town of St. Anthony. With that, he wished me good luck, told me he would see me in St. John's after the election, and left. For the remainder of the 21-day campaign, I was on my own.

Nineteen

Campaigning among the Mourners

Joseph R. Smallwood always maintained a healthy respect for the churches and the political influence of their leaders. He never hesitated to take on union leaders when provoked, or the business community or municipal leaders—for that matter, any other organization or group if he thought it justified. But he always gave the churches a wide berth, never doing or saying anything that would offend their leaders.

The evening before we were to leave St. John's to kick off my 1962 campaign, Smallwood invited me to his office, where he gave me a crash course in Newfoundland politics. He stressed the importance of paying courtesy calls on the clergy as soon as I arrived in a community, "always in the order of their numbers and the relative size of their congregations," he said. "For example, in St. Anthony the largest single denomination is the United Church. Therefore, you must call on the United Church minister first. In Englee most of the people belong to the Salvation Army, and in Conche all the people are Roman Catholic." He suggested that I visit Conche early in the campaign and spend some time with Father McCormick, whose parish included Conche, Croque and Goose Cove. It seemed an unorthodox way of conducting a political campaign, but if that's what it took to get elected, I was prepared to try it—at least once. Surely it couldn't hurt, and it might even help, in some way I hadn't considered.

Smallwood reminded me that the Apostolic Faith was strong in Roddickton, where it had been first introduced to Newfoundland in 1951 by Pastor Stanley Hancock. Smallwood suggested that I pay my respects to Hancock as soon as I arrived in Roddickton. I wondered how the good pastor would feel about my sudden appearance but managed to shrug off my misgivings. Certainly—here I reminded myself of my earlier thought on the matter—it couldn't hurt.

I spent several days stormbound in the St. Anthony area, powerless to do anything more than wait out the weather—a frustrating wait. I was eager to campaign. However, the weather soon cleared and, using the small aircraft that had been assigned to me, I instructed its pilot to set out for Roddickton where I would pay my respects to Pastor Hancock.

I was met at the door of the pastor's home by a lady who led me into the living room where I found the pastor seated at an old desk preparing a sermon for a funeral service the next day. He seemed very much the salt of the earth: a sturdy older man with a studious air about him. He told me that the deceased was a young logger who was killed in an accident the previous day in the woods near Roddickton.

I told the pastor, "Premier Smallwood sends his regards and asked me to thank you in advance for any help you give me in my campaign."

The 63-year-old pastor, who looked and spoke like an evangelist, laid down his pen and, in a quivering voice, said, "Yes, Brother Carter, I will help you, maybe when you least expect it. Please tell my dear old friend, Mr. Smallwood, that my prayers are with him. I will do all I can to get you and the Liberal Party elected."

The Pastor's response was better than I had expected. I was glad that I'd taken Smallwood's advice; it seemed to me that this impromptu visit was the best thing that I could have done.

I did not want to prolong my visit as it was getting late, and I knew the pastor had work to do. "Thank you for seeing me," I told him, "and for your offer of support." As I started to walk towards the front door, he called me back into the room. I hesitated, wondering what more he might possibly have to say.

Looking up from his desk, he gave me a sly wink and whispered, "God moves in mysterious ways, Brother Carter. Be sure to attend the funeral of our dear departed brother tomorrow afternoon. Your presence will provide great solace to the family."

I wasn't certain what sort of solace I might be able to provide—I certainly didn't know the young logger, or his family—and I admit that I was curious as to what the Pastor intended. "I'll be there," I assured him.

As I approached the church the next day, I was surprised to see people actually lined up, waiting to enter. A moment or two after I took my place in the line-up, Pastor Hancock eyed me standing in the crowd. He came over to me and, without saying a word, took me by the arm and led me inside the church. Ignoring my obvious embarrassment, he literally dragged me to the front of the church and seated me in the pew reserved for the family of the deceased. I was mortified, wondering what the rest of the congregation thought, especially the family. Yet there seemed no sure way to make my escape. I would have to remain here, despite my discomfort, and hope that my presence was not seen as an intrusion into the family's private grief.

I have always had a terrible aversion to attending wakes. It was just one of those things that made me supremely uncomfortable and ill at ease.

As a young lad, I idolized my grandfather Carter. When he died in the late 1930s, I was devastated. As was the custom in those days, he was laid out in the front room of our home. For three days I avoided going near that room. On the day of the funeral, my parents insisted that I take one last look at my grandfather in his coffin—despite my own considerable apprehensions. It was respectful to do so, I knew, and yet I could not reconcile the body in the coffin with the vibrant life that my grandfather had led. Seeing him there affected me terribly and, for twenty years, I avoided attending wakes.

Obviously, Pastor Hancock had no way of knowing my aversion to being around corpses. The pew in which I was seated was no more than three feet from the open casket. I felt very uncomfortable and ill at ease. At first, I avoided looking at the deceased. I tried to sit sideways on the pew and look the other way. However, when the mourners arrived, my bench was so crowded I had to sit up straight and, as a result, could not avoid facing the open casket.

By the time the service was ready to start, the church was filled to capacity. All the pews were filled, and people were standing in the aisles and at the back of the building. Pastor Hancock was an extremely emotional preacher. An old-time, fire-and-brimstone evangelist, he seemed to be at his best in front of a full church. In his sermon, which lasted for at least 45 minutes, he pulled no punches in describing hell and the ultimate fate of those who "do not live by the Book."

The congregation was very responsive. At times, shouts of "Amen" and "Praise the Lord" drowned out the pastor as he recited passages from the Bible to back up his assurances to the family of the deceased that they had nothing to worry about as far as their departed loved one was concerned. It was a moving service. Even though I did not know the deceased or the family, at times I found myself fighting back tears. The evangelical tremor in the pastor's voice, the solemnity of his message and the grief of the mourners took their toll on my emotions.

A few minutes before Pastor Hancock concluded his sermon, he paused and looked my way. My presence in the church obviously reminded him of his promise to me: that he would help me with my election. I was soon to find out what he meant when he said, "maybe when you least expect it."

"My friends," he said, "we are honoured today to have in

our midst, seated in the front row with the family of the deceased, our Liberal candidate, Mr. Carter. Stand up, Mr. Carter, and let your future constituents see you." Raising his voice to be heard over shouts of "Amen" and "Hallelujah" from the congregation, he reminded them of the many blessings bestowed on them by Premier Smallwood and the Liberal government: free drugs, free hospitalization and free medical care.

Still having to raise his voice to be heard over the shouts from the congregation, he continued, "Those of us who were around during the dirty thirties, and had to keep body and soul together on six cents a day, know and appreciate what Mr. Smallwood and the Liberal Party have done for us. How many of you remember what it was like before Mr. Smallwood brought us into Confederation? Raise you hands and say 'Amen'!" Every hand in the church shot up as the entire congregation shouted "Amen! Hallelujah!" It was an astonishing spectacle.

"In conclusion," the pastor said, "I want to thank Mr. Carter, on your behalf, for having the interest to be here with us today. I know I speak for the family of our dear departed brother, and for all of you, when I say that we look forward to having Mr. Carter represent us in the House of Assembly."

When the service concluded, the pallbearers closed the casket and moved it to the centre aisle of the church. The pastor then called the order of the procession to the grave-yard. "We must now take our dear departed brother to his final resting place," he said. "Would the wife and mother of the deceased, and our Liberal candidate, Mr. Carter, take their place in that order directly behind the casket? Would the other mourners please fall in behind Mr. Carter?"

Twenty

The L'Anse Aux Meadows Fiasco

During the first two weeks of the 1962 campaign, the weather on the Great Northern Peninsula was terrible, with rain, drizzle and fog every day. Since all but a few of the communities were isolated and inaccessible by road, I had to rely on a small, float-equipped aircraft provided by the Liberal Party. The pilot was a young man from Cape Breton who had absolutely no experience flying around the Newfoundland coast. In fact, this was his first job.

Flying conditions on the tip of the Great Northern Peninsula are tricky at the best of times. With the prevailing winds blowing on land from the northeast, the seas are usually too rough and the winds too strong for small aircraft to land. Campaigning in White Bay North was not easy, especially in the fall, hampered as we were by both bad weather and a pilot whose inexperience and lack of knowledge of the Newfoundland coast made him overly cautious.

In the more sheltered communities, we were able to land on the harbour and taxi to the government wharf, where the people would be gathered to meet their Liberal candidate, more commonly referred to by the local residents as "Joey's man." In practically every community, the mere mention of Smallwood's name appeared to have a mystical effect on people. In almost every home I visited, there was a picture of Smallwood hanging on the wall, flanked by a picture of King William of Orange or a member of the royal family, or a religious picture.

With less than a week left in the campaign and still no

improvement in the weather, I had to take advantage of every hour of suitable flying weather to campaign in the more isolated communities. In cases where it was impossible to land on the harbour waters, we would fly over the community at a very low altitude and, using the public address system strapped to the plane's undercarriage, I would speak to the people as they gathered in groups on the ground. It was not the best way to campaign, especially in a district in which you were a complete stranger, but I had no choice.

Usually after we circled the community a few times, with music blaring from the loudspeakers, people would come from their homes to see what all the racket was about. For many White Bay North residents, this was the first time they were exposed to such campaigning. When I was satisfied that everybody in the community was aware of my presence, I would speak on the loudspeaker, repeating the Liberal campaign slogan which, in that election, was, "Help for those who can't work...jobs for those who can." We would circle the community for as long as it took me to deliver my message and ask the people to give me their vote.

Even though it sometimes took several passes over a community to deliver my message, the actions of the people below convinced me that it was getting through and was being favourably received. They step-danced to the music from the public address system and waved their arms as we flew over.

There were times, though, when their reaction was somewhat less than favourable—perhaps not to my message but certainly to the manner in which it was being delivered. The noise and confusion of an airplane skimming over the rooftops with music blaring was not only disconcerting for the elderly and infirm, it also played havoc with the animals, especially dogs and horses. Flying over one community, I saw an old farmer walking a pair of horses across a field towards a barn. The engine noise and the music scared the horses and caused them to bolt. They galloped across a field, leaving the poor fellow standing there, probably as scared and confused as the horses were. As we made a second pass over the community, I saw the horses still galloping towards open country with the farmer in hot pursuit.

Aware of the construction project underway in L'Anse Aux Meadows, I wanted to spend some time there meeting the workers, most of whom were from nearby communities and who would be voting in the White Bay North District. Situated on the northeast tip of the Great Northern Peninsula, L'Anse Aux Meadows was not your ordinary Newfoundland fishing outport. Inaccessible by road until the 1970s, it gained international attention in 1960, when Norwegian archaeologists Helge and Anne Ingstad excavated a Viking settlement they subsequently identified as the winter station of Leif Eriksson in 1000 A.D. It was declared a national historic park in 1968 and a world heritage site a decade later.

Funded by the Government of Canada, work on the L'Anse Aux Meadows site commenced early in 1962, and was at its peak when I campaigned there in mid-November. Since most of the men who worked on the project were from the small, isolated communities that dotted the coastline, getting them all together in one area was more than I had hoped for.

By the time we arrived over L'Anse Aux Meadows, the wind had come up from the northeast and was blowing a gale. The pilot would not take a chance on landing on the harbour because of the high winds and rough seas. Still anxious to make contact with the people below, I instructed the pilot to circle the area. I would again use the loudspeaker to speak to them from the air. As we flew over, there were thirty or forty men working on the roof of a huge temporary building that was being constructed over the entire archaeological site to protect it from the weather and make it possible for the archaeologists to continue working during the winter.

Obviously, the workmen were anxious to take advantage of the fine weather too, because they were out in force that day, trying to cover the roof before the bad weather set in for the winter. To attract their attention, I increased the volume of the loudspeaker, put on an Irish jig, and flew over the site several times. At the appropriate time, I used the speaker to deliver my message and ask the people on the ground for their support. Evidently, my message was being well received, for the men on the roof waved their arms, step-danced to the music, and threw their caps and other articles of clothing in the air. They were a most responsive audience.

With my enthusiasm getting the better of me, I told the pilot to fly out to sea, then come in at an even lower altitude and make another pass over the site. I wanted to make sure that every person in the community, especially the men working on the roof, knew I was in the area. We flew about five miles out to sea, swung around, and approached the land just above sea level. With the public address system spewing out an Irish jig, we headed straight for the building.

When they saw us coming, the men on the roof went wild. Again, they jumped up and down, waved their arms, and threw things in the air.

What a great way to campaign! I thought. It sure beats knocking on doors.

Suddenly, something was wrong—the workers on the roof seemed to have panicked. Apparently, the horror of what they thought was about to happen hit all of them at the same time. As we approached the building, flying barely above sea-level, they thought we were going to land on the roof.

In the few seconds that it took to approach and fly over the site, we saw people going everywhere. Some scrambled to the edge of the roof and jumped off. Others threw themselves onto the roof and lay flat on their stomachs, afraid to move. Fortunately, it was a one-story building with a flat roof. I dread to think what would have happened had it been a taller building.

As soon as he could, the pilot veered the plane around and flew back over the site to see what had happened. It was not a very encouraging sight. Below us we saw a bunch of men running as fast as they could to get away from the building. Those who remained on the roof were getting to their feet, brushing themselves off, angrily shaking their fists and making threatening gestures at us.

"Head back to St. Anthony," I told the pilot. "We've done enough damage for one day." I was convinced that not only was I ruined politically, but that I would end up in court with a couple of dozen lawsuits on my hands.

Twenty-one

A Visit to the District

Following the election I lost no time returning to the district and getting to know the people and familiarizing myself with their problems. Getting there, however, wasn't easy. Although the road to the Peninsula was officially opened by Premier Smallwood during the election campaign, sections of it weren't completed until the following year.

People wishing to travel to the Great Northern Peninsula in those days had two choices. They could use the Canadian National Coastal Boat service, which provided a weekly passenger and freight service from Lewisporte to the larger communities along the northern coasts and operated from early spring to late fall. Or, they could use a regular single-engine aircraft to get as far as St. Anthony, where there was a small airstrip, then go by float-equipped aircraft to outlying communities.

The St. Anthony airstrip was started in 1957. For years it was referred to as "McCormick's Field," after Father McCormick, a Roman Catholic priest in the area whose intense lobbying was instrumental in having the facility built. However, it was not equipped to handle regularly scheduled, third-level air carriers until 1981.

The first leg of our journey to White Bay North after the election was by boat. As soon as navigation opened that spring, Muriel and I boarded the coastal boat in Lewisporte and headed to St. Anthony, where we spent several days attending social functions, making new friends, and developing a relationship with community and church leaders. We then set out in a small, float-equipped aircraft to visit the dozen or so communities inaccessible by road.

One of the first communities we visited was St. Anthony Bight, a small fishing community located about six miles northeast of St. Anthony.

Although the first permanent settlers arrived in the area in the 1850s, St. Anthony Bight remained isolated until the mid-1960s, when it was connected by road to other communities on the Great Northern Peninsula, including St. Anthony. Except for a few walking trails over bogs and unsurveyed terrain, there were no real roads until that time.

The winds of change that swept with hurricane force over most of rural Newfoundland and Labrador in the wake of Confederation were generated mainly by Smallwood's frantic determination to end isolation, and catapult Newfoundlanders and Labradorians into the twentieth century. It started with a massive road construction program, opening up hundreds of isolated communities. Tens of thousands of people who for decades had lived in total isolation suddenly found themselves caught up in the hustle and bustle of an entirely different lifestyle.

The people of St. Anthony Bight were no exception. After more than a century of isolation, the doors to the twentieth century suddenly burst open and a deluge of motor vehicles carrying long-forgotten friends, absentee family members and, in many cases, strangers, invaded the community. Some residents readily adjusted to the change, but others found it extremely difficult to overcome their inhibitions and communicate with outsiders. But when I first visited there as MHA, such change was yet to come.

My visit to St. Anthony Bight as a new MHA was a stark reminder of the curse of isolation and the terrible impact it had on our people, especially older members of a community. The pilot of our small, single-engine aircraft landed on a pond near St. Anthony Bight. My wife and I walked the short distance to the community, where we slowly strolled around and met the people. Most of them were working in their gardens or simply standing around to catch a glimpse of the new Member and his "Missus."

While we were walking around, I noticed a woman—perhaps middle-aged—following us. She wore a long, shabby black smock and had a black bandanna tightly secured under her chin. Whenever I turned around and tried to talk to her, she put her hand over her mouth and walked away. Obviously, she wanted to get my attention but was unable to build up the courage.

Everywhere we went, the woman in black followed us. When we entered a house to visit, she would be standing around when we came out and would run in the opposite direction when I approached her. This continued for a couple of hours. Finally, as we were winding up our visit and returning to the plane, Muriel suggested that I make one last attempt to reach the woman, since she obviously wanted to speak to me about something. She must have realized that this was her last opportunity to capture my attention before we left because this time, as I approached her, she stood her ground. Holding one hand over her mouth, she gestured with her other hand for us to follow her into a nearby house.

Without uttering a word, she led us into the kitchen where four small, poorly dressed children were sitting around an old cast-iron woodstove from which a rusty, worn-out tin stovepipe was belching smoke and flankers through the roof. However, not all the smoke made it through the roof; some of it escaped along the way through the holes in the stovepipe and remained in the kitchen.

With tears running down my cheeks, and trying desperately to control a fit of coughing brought on by the smoke, I used all sorts of hand gestures to ask the woman if she had a problem she wished to discuss with me. Her only response was to place one hand over her mouth and, with her other hand, point towards the stove. She was obviously trying to tell me that she needed a new stove. Motioning for me to inspect the stove, she pointed to its worn-out funnel and twisted grating.

Lacking the ability to communicate in sign language, I tried to emulate a bird in flight. Like an amateur pantomimist, I stood in the middle of the kitchen—still coughing and with my eyes watering—and went through all kinds of physical contortions as I struggled to communicate with her. I flapped my arms and mouthed the words, "When I fly back to St. John's, I will see the man with the bow-tie in Confederation Building [Premier Smallwood] and get you a new stove."

With her hand still held tightly over her mouth, she nodded her head, appearing to understand what I was trying to tell her.

Thinking that perhaps she could read my lips, between coughs I slowly mouthed the question, "Is there anything else I can do for you?"

Looking somewhat confused, she pointed to the children around the stove, who were obviously getting a great kick out of my antics.

Again flapping my arms like a bird in flight and making the same gestures with my hands, I repeated the entire exercise. "When I fly back to St. John's, I will talk to the man with the bow-tie in Confederation Building and get clothing for your children."

After twenty or so minutes standing in the middle of the kitchen flapping my arms, coughing and making various hand gestures, I tried to tell the woman I had to go. We had to visit several other communities before nightfall. With the four children clinging to their mother's worn-out, ill-fitting smock, she followed me to the door.

As we were leaving, I turned around and again gestured with my hands, trying to assure her that I would do my best to get assistance for her and her children. I pointed towards the pond where the plane was waiting, again flapping my arms and trying to tell her I had to leave. With mixed emotions, Muriel and I walked away from the house in complete silence. What we had just witnessed had a sobering effect on both of us.

Suddenly, as we were approaching the road, I couldn't believe my ears. In a loud, almost hysterical voice, I heard the woman shouting, "Good-bye, Mr. Carter. Good-bye, Missus."

Looking around, I saw her and her children standing in the doorway, frantically waving their arms and shouting their good-byes.

Twenty-two

Among the Honourable Members

The outcome of the 1962 election held few surprises. Despite the protestations of others to the contrary, there was never any doubt that the Liberals would win—the betting was on the size of their majority.

The only real surprise in the election results was the upsurge in Tory support, especially in the rural areas, where they won three seats and came close to winning several others. In total, the Progressive Conservative Party elected seven members in that election, including four seats in St. John's—their greatest number since Confederation. The Liberals elected thirty-four members. Smallwood was re-elected in Bonavista North, where he defeated his Progressive Conservative opponent by more than four to one.

One independent was elected: Charlie Devine in Labrador West. In that election, the United Newfoundland Party ran one candidate, Gus Duffy, who lost his bid for re-election in the District of St. John's Centre to Progressive Conservative Ank Murphy. John O'Dea, one of the founding members of the United Newfoundland Party, joined the Liberals before the election and was narrowly defeated in St. John's South by Progressive Conservative G. Rex Renouf. O'Dea was the author of his own misfortune. During the campaign he was caught handing out "pink slips" to some of his less fortunate constituents, who later redeemed them at the local store for a week's groceries. O'Dea's good intentions were construed by his opponent as "buying votes," and the resulting furore cost him the election.

Three members of the St. John's City Council were elected as Liberals in that election: Bill Adams in St. John's West; Geoff Carnell in St. John's North; and myself in White Bay North. Councillors Jim Fagan and Jim Higgins narrowly lost in St. John's East Extern and St. John's East, respectively, to the Tory candidates. Adams served until 1965, when he resigned his seat and successfully contested the mayoral race in the 1965 St. John's municipal election. Carnell served one term in the Legislature but did not seek re-election. Higgins was appointed to the Newfoundland Supreme Court, and Fagan remained on the city council.

One of the Tories elected was Ambrose Peddle. A long-time Conservative, he was enjoying considerable popularity as mayor of Windsor, his adopted home town, when he successfully contested the Grand Falls district. Peddle was one of the three Tory members elected in 1962 in districts outside St. John's, which heralded the dissolution of Small-wood's political hold on rural Newfoundlanders and Labradorians.

Peddle was noted for his sense of humour and dry wit. An ultra-conservative, he had very little tolerance for theatrics or political showmanship, particularly when it came from the government side of the House. Liberal backbencher Uriah Strickland, the MHA for Trinity South, was proving that he was good at political showmanship and theatrics as he took part in the first Throne Speech debate following the 1962 election. A master mariner and a devout member of the Salvation Army, Uriah attended the Number Two Salvation Army Citadel on Adelaide Street in St. John's, where he served for several years as the Corps Sergeant Major. Strickland possessed considerable personal ambition. As a Salvationist, he felt that he had almost a divine right to a Cabinet portfolio in the Smallwood administration. "Not for myself, mind you," he would hasten to add, "but for the Salvation Army; they deserve to have one of their own in Cabinet."

Perceiving himself to be a great orator, Strickland did not fail to take advantage of the latitude accorded backbenchers in the Throne Speech debate to impress the House, especially the Premier. Whenever Uriah Strickland rose to participate in a debate in the House of Assembly, however, he did not merely speak—-he roared.

After the customary congratulations to the newly elected members of the Legislature and to "Canada's most distinguished Premier on another well-deserved electoral victory," Strickland quickly got into high gear. Citing passages from Holy Writ interspersed with paragraphs from the Liberal Manifesto, he ranted and roared for the full 45-minute period allotted to private members.

Sitting across the Chamber from the official Opposition, I could see that the rookie Member for Grand Falls was not impressed. Judging by the expression on his face, the content of Strickland's speech and the patronizing way in which it was delivered were taking their toll on Ambrose Peddle. Unlike some of his more boisterous colleagues, however, he accorded Strickland the time-honoured parliamentary privilege of being heard in silence. Finally, there was a sigh of relief from both sides of the House when the Speaker stood and called Strickland to order: "The Honourable Member's time has expired," he said. "Would he please be seated." Reluctantly, Strickland concluded his speech and was about to take his seat when Peddle shouted in a voice loud enough for all to hear, "And they called the wind Uriah!"

Strickland's reaction to this waggish retort has not been recorded.

Twenty-three

Remembering Billy Browne

Since first entering public life, I have met and known personally most of the people engaged in politics on the Newfoundland scene and many on the national scene. I have known on a first-name basis six Newfoundland Premiers, five Prime Ministers of Canada, and four Governors-General. I served in Cabinet under three Premiers, one Liberal and two Tories, and survived in the provincial fisheries portfolio for nine years. Of all the politicians I have known, there aren't any for whom I have greater respect than the Honourable William J. (Billy) Browne.

In every sense of the word, Billy Browne was a gentleman and a scholar. Born in St. John's in 1897, Browne was admitted to the Bar of England in 1922, and subsequently to the Newfoundland Bar as a solicitor. He was first elected to the House of Assembly in 1924. During his political career, he was elected in the provincial districts of St. John's West, Harbour Main-Bell Island, St. John's South and St. John's East Extern. In 1949 he was elected to the Canadian House of Commons in St. John's West, and re-elected in the 1957 and 1958 general elections. Following the 1958 federal election, he was appointed to the Diefenbaker Cabinet, and in 1960 he became Solicitor General of Canada.

Smallwood's dislike for Browne was exceeded only by his hatred for John Diefenbaker who, as Canada's Prime Minister in the late 1950s, crossed swords with Smallwood over several issues affecting Newfoundland. It was with the Diefenbaker administration that Newfoundland had one of its bit-

terest constitutional disputes, over the stand taken by Diefenbaker on Term 29 of the Terms of Union between Newfoundland and Canada. Allowing for any financial consequences to
Newfoundland upon becoming a province of Canada, Term
29 obligated the Government of Canada to appoint a Royal
Commission within eight years of the date of union to review
Newfoundland's financial position.

Under the Terms of Union, during the first twelve years
of union Newfoundland would receive a transitional grant to
help it adjust to its status as a province of Canada. While these
grants were paid on a declining scale and would cease after
twelve years, it was agreed in 1949 that there could be no
finality to such an arrangement. At the end of the first eight

years of Confederation, the Canadian government would set up a Royal Commission to review the province's financial situation. It would also recommend the amount of assistance needed to enable the province to provide and maintain public services comparable to those prevailing in the Maritime provinces, without having to resort to more burdensome taxation.

Before the eight years were up, Smallwood jumped the gun. Not content to leave it to the federal government to assess Newfoundland's entitlement under Term 29, in 1956 he appointed a Newfoundland Royal Commission to prepare its own case for additional financial assistance—under the chairmanship of St. John's Lawyer Philip J. Lewis, a sitting Member of the House of Assembly and a Minister without portfolio in the Smallwood Cabinet. The Newfoundland Royal Commission suggested that the province should receive $15 million a year in federal grants, in perpetuity, to help Newfoundland and Labrador catch up with the rest of the Atlantic Provinces.

The Royal Commission appointed by the federal government in the fall of 1957 and headed by J. B. McNair, a former Premier of New Brunswick, saw things differently. In July 1958, ignoring the report of the Newfoundland Royal Commission, the McNair Royal Commission recommended that the grant be kept at the original eight million dollars a year until 1962, when the province's financial position would be further reviewed. Diefenbaker lost no time accepting the McNair recommendation.

Diefenbaker was not content to have ignored the recommendation of the Newfoundland Royal Commission. On the eve of Newfoundland's tenth anniversary as a province, he announced that all financial assistance to Newfoundland under Term 29 would be discontinued after 1962, and that the monies paid to that time would be a "final and irrevocable settlement" of the Canadian government's obligation to Newfoundland under the Terms of Union.

Smallwood was outraged. His first official response to Diefenbaker's announcement was to declare three days of official mourning and to issue an order that all flags on government buildings fly at half-mast. Carrying placards demanding that Newfoundland secede from Confederation, hundreds of university students led by individuals dressed as undertakers paraded around St. John's behind a black coffin as a band played the Funeral March.

"Secession is not the answer!" Smallwood shouted as he addressed them on the front steps of Confederation Building. "Our quarrel is not with the people of Canada; it's John Diefenbaker who betrayed us." After he assured the students that the rest of Canada was ready to rise up in rebellion against Diefenbaker, they left to burn Canada's Prime Minister in effigy. Smallwood then started on a nationwide campaign to change the federal government's ruling and defeat John Diefenbaker.

Smallwood tried his best to encourage Browne to break with Diefenbaker and the federal Tories on the Term 29 issue. However, Browne remained loyal to his Party, continuing to serve in the Diefenbaker Cabinet. Smallwood's contempt for both Diefenbaker and Browne was unrelenting. In the 1962 federal election, Smallwood worked like a man possessed, in his determination to unseat Browne in St. John's West. Within hours of the election call, Smallwood mobilized the entire provincial Liberal machine and, like a general preparing for battle, meticulously prepared the strategy for Browne's political demise.

I attended a meeting at the CLB Armoury in St. John's, where Smallwood and Liberal Party strategists Joe Ashley, Frank Wall and Ed Learning unveiled their new "poll captain" system, which would be used for the first time in Newfoundland in the St. John's West federal election campaign. Employing an army of workers, the plan was to canvass the entire constituency, identify the Liberal supporters, and ensure that on polling day they got out to vote. As I sat and listened to Smallwood and his three lieutenants outline their strategy for defeating Browne, I found myself feeling pity for the "poor old brute."

Smallwood was aided and abetted by the federal Liberals, including Opposition Leader Lester Pearson and Jack Pickersgill. They were quick to recognize the level of support Smallwood was getting across Canada in his crusade against Diefenbaker.

When the final election results were in, Liberal Richard Cashin won the St. John's West seat by 24 votes, and the Diefenbaker Government—that had won by a landslide in 1958—lost its majority in the House of Commons. It was forced into another general election a year later and was defeated.

Still smarting from the loss of his federal seat, Browne resurfaced on the Newfoundland political scene five months later, when he ran in the provincial election and won the St. John's East Extern seat for the Progressive Conservatives. People close to Smallwood sensed that he had mixed feelings about Browne's return to the House of Assembly in 1962. While he instinctively looked forward to an opportunity to taunt his old political adversary about his "former boss" John Diefenbaker, whom he characterized as "an enemy of Newfoundland," Smallwood knew that with Browne's capacity for work, his tenacity and political experience, the twenty-third General Assembly of Newfoundland's House of Assembly would be much more challenging and interesting than the previous one.

It was my privilege to sit across from Browne in the Newfoundland Legislature from 1962 to 1965. An ardent anti-confederate, Browne had vehemently opposed Newfoundland's union with Canada in 1949 because, he argued, it constituted a breach of trust on the part of the British government. Browne was a Minister in the Alderdice government when Responsible Government was suspended in 1934. His argument, supported by many Newfoundlanders, was based on a pledge by the British Government in 1933 that "when the Island's difficulties had been overcome and the country was again self-supporting, Responsible Government, on request from the people of Newfoundland, would be restored."

For the next three years, Smallwood and Browne fought like cats. Smallwood never missed an opportunity to remind Newfoundlanders and Labradorians that "Billy Browne is a friend of John Diefenbaker, the man who betrayed Newfoundland on Term 29." Whenever Browne tried to defend Diefenbaker's actions, Smallwood would say, "Friends of my enemies are my enemies, too."

With the tenacity of a pit bull, Browne was undoubtedly one of the most effective Opposition members who ever sat in the Newfoundland House of Assembly. A prodigious worker and able debater, he was at his best when the budget and the spending estimates were examined in the Legislature, especially when time was running out on the Interim Supply Bill that had to be approved by the Legislature before March 31, the end of the government's fiscal year.

Browne's training at Oxford University, where he studied law as a Rhodes Scholar, and his subsequent 14-year tenure as a Newfoundland District Court Judge, served him well as a member of the official Opposition.

Much to their discomfort, Browne interrogated Smallwood and his Ministers as though they were guilty of some heinous crime, and in a manner reminiscent of his days on the bench. He tenaciously questioned each item of government expenditure and, in the same tone of voice that struck fear in the heart of many a poor old St. John's drunk who appeared before him in Magistrate's Court, he demanded detailed explanations from Smallwood and his Ministers.

It was only after Smallwood's departure in 1972 that the daily oral question period was instituted in the Newfoundland House of Assembly. Even though a daily question period is a long-established item in the Standing Orders of the House of Commons in the United Kingdom, Ottawa and all other Canadian provincial legislatures, Smallwood would have nothing to do with it during his twenty-three years as Premier. He was not about to make it easy for Opposition Members to ask questions.

With his experience as a Member of the Canadian House of Commons and a Minister in the Diefenbaker government, Browne knew firsthand what it was like to be grilled and cross-examined daily by the Opposition. He was also aware of the advantages it gave the Opposition and the attention it received from the media. A daily barrage of hard-hitting, well-orchestrated questions by Opposition Members Jack Pickersgill, Paul Martin, Allan McEacten and Lester Pearson, known in the House of Commons as "the four horsemen of the Apocalypse," was a major contributor to Diefenbaker's defeat in 1963.

Despite the absence of a daily question period in the Newfoundland House of Assembly, Browne availed of every opportunity to ask embarrassing questions of Smallwood and his Ministers. One such opportunity presented itself just as the House commenced an afternoon sitting shortly after the 1962 election. Browne's question to the Premier concerned a study into civil servants' pensions, commissioned earlier by the Smallwood government. It was chaired by a former chairman of the Public Service Commission and Deputy Minister of Natural Resources, Kenneth J. Carter. Browne wanted to know why it was taking Carter so long to complete the study and report back to the Legislature. Since the Minister responsible for reporting to the House on matters affecting the Public Service Commission, Myles Murray (Minister of Provincial Affairs) was not present, Browne directed his question to the Premier.

Following a lengthy preamble and charges that Smallwood had commissioned the study for political reasons, Browne asked: "Why is the Premier dragging his feet on this very important matter?"

Smallwood knew that, following an old, unwritten custom that is still adhered to by Opposition Members, Browne would never ask a question in the House of Assembly unless he already knew the answer. What is the old fox up to now? Smallwood thought as he stood to reply to Browne's question. Smallwood was not about to give his arch political enemy the satisfaction of receiving a straight answer. "After all," he would say, "if members of the Opposition, especially Browne, get into the habit of asking questions and getting answers in the Legislature, there is no telling where it will end. Before we know it, they'll be demanding a daily question period like they got in the House of Commons."

Determined to frustrate Browne, Smallwood went through the motions of responding to his question. He acknowledged the existence of the report, but he would not give Browne the satisfaction of an answer. Instead, he talked endlessly of the virtues of its author, Kenneth J. Carter, and the dedication of the Minister whose responsibility it was to act on its recommendations. He characterized Carter as an outstanding Newfoundlander. He gave the Legislature a full account of Carter's war record. "Having distinguished himself on the battlefields of Europe in the First Great War," he said, "he returned to civilian life in 1918, to distinguish himself again, this time in the public service of Newfoundland."

Several times during Smallwood's protracted discourse on Carter's merits, Browne asked the Speaker to instruct the

Premier to get to the point, "Where is the Carter Commission's report on civil service pensions?"

Speakers of the Newfoundland House of Assembly showed great reluctance to interrupt Smallwood while he was speaking, even when he was out of order. Consequently, Smallwood rambled on, carefully avoiding saying anything that would be of value to Browne.

Finally, realizing that Smallwood was playing games and had no intention of answering his question, Browne exploded, "Mr. Speaker, if you are not prepared to bring order to this House and name the Premier for abusing its privileges, I will withdraw my question and keep it for when the Minister responsible for the Civil Service Commission takes his seat."

Smallwood agreed that the question should have been put to the Honourable Minister in the first place, "because he is in a much better position to provide the Honourable Member with an answer." He then went on to extol the virtues of the Minister of Provincial Affairs, Myles Murray. After accusing Browne of wasting the time of the House by his "constant interjections," Smallwood said, "The Honourable Minister has had the report of the Carter Commission in his possession for several weeks and knows it off by heart." He went on to say that he and Murray had already discussed it at length and that he "marvelled at the extent to which the Minister has absorbed its contents. I keep asking myself how in God's name the Minister gets the time to do it. Not only has he read and reread the Carter report, he also understands completely the implications of its recommendations and their cost to the treasury."

As Smallwood was getting ready to wind up, Murray, who was noted for his extended "liquid lunches," entered the Chamber and took his seat.

Browne again rose on a point of order to remind the Speaker that the Minister of Provincial Affairs was in the

Chamber, and would he now order the Premier to take his seat and allow the Minister to respond to his question.

Taken completely by surprise and unaware of how Small-wood had handled the question, Murray asked the Speaker which report the Member was talking about. Browne repeated his question.

Looking at Smallwood for some indication of how to deal with the question, and obviously feeling the effects of his "lunch," Murray fumbled for an answer. "There are so many reports coming over my desk these days, Mr. Speaker," he said, "it's a job to keep up with them. What report is he talking about, Mr. Speaker?"

"He knows very well which report I am talking about, Mr. Speaker," Browne said. "It's the Carter Commission report on civil service pensions. Will he now answer my question?"

By this time, Murray smelled a rat. He knew Browne was up to no good. Still stalling and hoping for a hint from Smallwood as to how to deal with the question, Murray again asked which report the Honourable Member was talking about.

By this time, Browne's patience was at a breaking point. He interjected, "You know very well which report I am referring to, the Carter report on civil service pensions. What has happened to it?"

"The Carter report," said a flustered Murray. "Oh, I see. You mean the Carter report on pensions."

Browne shouted, "Yes, the Carter report on Civil Service pensions. What action do you intend to take on the recommendations, and how much will it cost?"

Trying to appear relieved that Browne had finally made himself clear, Murray said, "Oh, that report. The Honourable Member's questions are not only garbled, but they are also premature, Mr. Speaker. I have not yet received that report, let alone read it."

While this exchange was taking place, all eyes in the

Legislature were on Smallwood as he squirmed in his seat, unable to do anything to avoid what he knew was going to be an embarrassment, and no doubt a prolonged series of points of order by Browne and charges that the Premier had deliberately misled the House. By the time Murray finished answering Browne's question, Smallwood's head was barely visible over the back of his seat. He knew the consequences of lying to another Honourable Member and deliberately misleading the House. He would have to apologize to the House. And—worse—he would have to apologize to Billy Browne.

Twenty-four

At Odds with the Skipper

Bill Adams' resignation in 1965 left St. John's West without representation. With at least a year to go before another provincial election, Smallwood was anxious to call a by-election to fill the vacant seat. The fortunes of the Liberal Party were showing signs of slipping, and Smallwood knew that the timing of the by-election and the selection of a candidate would have to be carefully considered. He did not want to risk losing the district to the Tories, who were gaining ground all over the province as a result of their successes in the 1962 general election.

A few days after Adams resigned, I received a telephone call from Smallwood, asking me to come to his office. He wanted to discuss something with me, he said. Getting off the elevator on the eighth floor of the Confederation Building, I met Muriel Templeman in the hall. She told me to go directly to the Premier's office, where he was waiting. As I entered, Smallwood and several key party strategists (including one of his most trusted political advisers, Joe Ashley) were sitting around talking. Obviously, their discussion was not meant for my ears because there was complete silence the moment I entered. I had the uncomfortable feeling that they were discussing a matter that involved me, and my sudden unannounced arrival had caught them by surprise. They seemed to be embarrassed as they waited for Smallwood to resume the discussion.

Pacing back and forth, his hands stuffed in his pants pockets, Smallwood immediately got down to business. He told us he was considering calling a by-election in St. John's West and he wanted the benefit of our advice. He stressed the importance of holding on to St. John's West, both to the Liberal Party and the Government. He spent the next ten or so minutes talking about the district and some of the political figures who had represented it in the House of Assembly, going back to the days of Responsible Government. He said it was the most prestigious district in the province. "In fact," he said, "because it is the district in which several Newfoundland Prime Ministers have been elected, including myself, it is always referred to as 'the Premier District.' "

Smallwood wanted to know how we felt about calling a by-election at that time. "What are the issues in the district, and how would a Liberal candidate make out if one were called?" he asked. To get our views on the first question, he went around the room and gave each of us an opportunity to express an opinion. It was generally agreed that, with the Tory party starting to show signs of coming alive, he should call the St. John's West by-election and get it over with as quickly as possible. As for the second part of his question—it was agreed that with the right candidate, winning the district would not be a problem. Adams was still popular, and his resignation to run for Mayor would not have a negative impact on the district or the Liberal Party's chance of retaining it.

Joe Ashley was the last person to respond to Smallwood's question. A lifelong resident of the city's west end, Ashley had an invaluable knowledge of the political situation in St. John's West. He knew most of the old-timers in the District on a first-name basis and could tell with incredible accuracy how they were leaning politically and what it would take to get them on side. All of us, including Smallwood, were anxiously waiting for Ashley to give us the benefit of his opinion.

Ashley agreed with the rest of us that an early by-election was advisable. However, he felt strongly that much would depend on the candidate. "With the right candidate," he said, "we can win the seat hands down." Whether it was coincidental or prearranged, it was obvious that Ashley was saying precisely what Smallwood wanted him to say.

When Ashley finished speaking, Smallwood agreed with his assessment of the situation. "You are absolutely right on both counts," he told Ashley. "We should call a by-election right away and, with the right candidate, we will win it hands down."

I had the feeling that this was not the first time the matter had been discussed by Smallwood and the others present. Everything was too well orchestrated, it seemed. Their assessment of the situation, Ashley's confidence that we would win, the emphasis he put on "the right candidate," and Smallwood's readiness to accept their advice left me with the uncomfortable feeling that the entire conversation had been carefully rehearsed. I knew then that the discussion taking place when I entered the room earlier was on the same subject. However, I remained unsure as to why they found it necessary to cut it off so abruptly when I entered. Obviously, the fact that Smallwood had invited me to the meeting meant that I would be privy to the matter under discussion and would in all likelihood be part of the campaign team.

Within minutes, things began to unfold. It started when I asked Smallwood, "Do you have anyone in mind to run in St. John's West if you decide to call the by-election?"

I was surprised that my question aroused so much interest; everybody in the room stopped talking and looked at me. Smallwood continued to pace the floor. As he was about to answer my question, he paused for a few seconds and walked over to where I was sitting. Motioning for me to stand, he reached out and took my hand. He shook it several times, then said, "You are our candidate."

I couldn't believe what I was hearing—surely he wasn't serious! Was he forgetting that I was already sitting in the

House of Assembly as the Member for White Bay North? I repeated my question, "In all seriousness, Mr. Premier, do you have someone in mind to run in St. John's West if and when a by-election is held?" He shot back with the same answer. "It's been agreed by the people in this room," he said, "including Joe Ashley—who knows St. John's West better than anyone in the Liberal Party—that *you* are one of the few people in the Party who can win the District."

I looked around the room for some indication from the others that this was just a joke, but all of them were serious.

I decided that Smallwood was not kidding. He actually wanted me to give up my seat in White Bay North, where I had been elected with a huge majority, and run in St. John's West. Even though I enjoyed campaigning and was certainly not averse to a good fight, if I did what Smallwood was asking me to do, how would I possibly explain it to the people of Newfoundland, particularly the people of White Bay North? I felt that I would be letting them down.

Smallwood was confident there would be no problem. "The people of White Bay North are good Liberals," he said. "They will do what I ask them to do if it's in the best interest of the Liberal Party. Look at what happened in the last election. You were a complete stranger, and they elected you with a whopping majority. I recall your telling me, when you and I arrived there back in 1962, that you did not know one person in the whole district. I took you there and asked them to send you back to the House of Assembly. The rest is history. Not only did they send you back to the House of Assembly, but they gave you the biggest majority of any Member elected in the election. In fact, I believe it is the largest majority received by a member since Confederation.

"As for rationalizing your actions in St. John's West, that should not pose a problem either. It is obvious that you have a strong desire to serve the people of St. John's; otherwise you would not be on the city council. As their representative in the

House of Assembly, sitting on the government side, you will be in a position to do a lot more for them and for the district than you would as a councillor. And it is equally obvious that you are a vote getter in St. John's. In 1961, almost completely unknown, you ran and won a seat on the council. According to the telephone polls I have had done, if you run for re-election in this year's municipal election, you will head the poll. You are by far the most popular person on the council."

At the time I took what Mr. Smallwood said with a grain of salt. However, in terms of my placement in the municipal council election two months later, he was close. I received considerably more votes than any of the incumbents. In that election, there were 26 people running for a seat on the six-member council. John Crosbie, who was running for the first time, headed the poll and was named Deputy Mayor. I came second.

Sensing that I was not overly enthusiastic, Smallwood suggested that I not make up my mind at that moment. "Take some time to think it over," he said, "and let me have your decision within a couple of days."

It did not take long for me to make up my mind. Despite Smallwood's opinion to the contrary, I knew that it would be difficult, if not impossible, to do what he had asked. The news media would have a field day at my expense. I decided that I simply couldn't subject myself to that.

I did not keep Smallwood waiting long for my decision. On Friday, a couple of days after our meeting, I telephoned Muriel Templeman and told her I wanted to see the Premier. She called me back a few minutes later and said, "Premier Smallwood will see you tomorrow at his home on Roaches Line."

Smallwood met me at the door and led me to his library, where he was rearranging and cataloguing a quantity of books he had just bought on the life of John Wesley. Smallwood went on at some length, telling me how he had managed to get his hands on the Wesley books, and that he now owned the largest collection of books on Wesley in Canada—perhaps even the world.

He seemed to be in a jovial mood, talking about his visits to Britain and the libraries and bookstores he had visited in search of rare books to add to his collection. It must have suddenly occurred to him why I was there. "Now, then," he said, "when am I going to be able to announce the date of the St. John's West by-election and your candidacy?"

I told him that I would not be able to do what he was asking of me. "Under different circumstances," I added, "I would consider it an honour to represent the people of St. John's West in the House of Assembly, but not this way. While I respect your opinion, and those of the other people who were in your office the other day, my instincts tell me that I would not be able to pull it off. The press and the Tory opposition would make mincemeat of me and my credibility."

Smallwood was not used to being turned down by anyone, least of all by a member of his own caucus. Obviously, he was unprepared for what he had just heard. Pausing for a few seconds, he proceeded to tell me, in no uncertain terms, how disappointed he was in me and my refusal to run in the by-election. He accused me of turning my back on him and the Liberal Party in their hour of need. As I was leaving, he became rather philosophical. "When you leave here today," he said, "you will be walking down a long, lonely road, all by yourself. You will not have me or the Liberal Party to help you—you will be alone."

It was certainly not one of my better moments. I had no doubt that I had made the right decision, but I knew that it would be a costly one. Smallwood had many noble qualities, but in such circumstances forgiveness was not one of them. When he was in his political heyday, it was unthinkable for a member of the caucus or a Cabinet Minister to "rebel" and leave the Party. Such an act was tantamount to burying one's political ambitions forever.

I did not know it then, but that meeting set the stage for one other meeting with Smallwood, the last time we would speak to each other for ten years. I would become a non-person, as far as Smallwood was concerned, and would remain that way until after the 1975 provincial election. At that time, I returned to provincial politics, subsequently entering the Moores Cabinet as Minister of Fisheries. In that election, Smallwood was elected in Twillingate District under the Liberal Reform Party that he had recently founded. We again became very good friends, and would often get together in his St. John's apartment for a meal and a chat about old times.

The by-election disagreement was not my first run-in with Smallwood. The first had occurred shortly after I was elected. In those days, it was customary to have the official opening of the House of Assembly take place on a Wednesday afternoon, a carry-over from when downtown businesses were closed on Wednesday afternoons and their workers given a half-day off. Back then, the official opening of the House of Assembly, with its pomp and circumstance, was an auspicious occasion. A large number of people, including downtown workers, lined up for hours to get a seat in the gallery, to hear the Governor read the Speech from the Throne and see their favourite politicians in action.

After the Lieutenant-Governor reads the Speech from the Throne and leaves the chamber, there are four other speeches on opening day. Two private government members speak for ten or fifteen minutes, moving and seconding the Address in Reply, followed by a speech by the Leader of the official Opposition and the Premier. The Premier usually speaks last and winds up the opening-day proceedings.

Moving and seconding the Address in Reply is an old parliamentary tradition, carried out by two private government members chosen by the Premier a couple of days in advance. Although the circumstances under which it came about left something to be desired, I was proud to have been selected by the Premier to move the Address in Reply in the 1963 session of the Legislature.

I first learned of this honour through the medium of my car radio as I was driving home to lunch. It was Monday afternoon, and Smallwood was being interviewed by a reporter, who asked him about the new session of the Legislature that was due to open on Wednesday. Smallwood gave a brief outline of the issues that would be debated during the new session, and the various bills that would be introduced. He concluded his interview by announcing the names of the government members who would be moving and seconding the Address in Reply on opening day. "The Honourable Member for White Bay North, Walter Carter, will be the mover of the Address in Reply, and Steve Neary, the Honourable Member for Bell Island, will be the seconder," he said.

When I arrived home, my wife told me that Premier Smallwood had been trying to reach me. He left word for me to call him as soon as I arrived. There were times when Smallwood could send your ego into a nose dive and, conversely, there were times when he had an uncanny way of making a person feel ten feet tall. It all depended on his mood and, of course, the circumstances that existed at the time.

When I got him on the phone that afternoon it was obvious that he was in a good mood and the circumstances were favourable. He started off our conversation by telling me that on Wednesday I would have an opportunity to make a place for myself in Newfoundland history. I was going to move the Address in Reply. He told me to come to his office later that afternoon to discuss the contents of my speech. "It is very important," he said, "that your speech be well prepared and that you be at your best when you read it. You will

be seen by tens of thousands of Newfoundlanders and Labradorians all over the province on live television."

Naturally, I was extremely pleased about the opportunity.

Later that afternoon I went to Smallwood's office to find
out if there was anything in particular he wanted me to
mention in my speech. I suggested to him that it would help
me develop a theme for my speech if I had an advance copy
of the proposed Speech from the Throne, which outlines in
general terms what the government hopes to achieve during
the ensuing session.

He appeared shocked by what I had said, and proceeded
to lecture me on the sanctity of the Speech from the Throne.
"It would be a terrible affront to Her Majesty the Queen if
anyone, other than His Honour the Lieutenant-Governor
and her first minister, the Premier, had access to the Speech
from the Throne before it was read by his Honour in the
Legislature. Nobody, but *nobody*, is given an advance copy of
His Honour's speech before it is read in the House of Assembly!"

Smallwood made me feel as if I were guilty of high treason
and close to being beheaded. I assured him that it was not my
intention to be disrespectful to Her Majesty the Queen or His
Honour the Lieutenant-Governor. I merely wanted to see
what the Speech from the Throne contained, in order to write
my speech around the same issues.

But Smallwood was emphatic. "You don't seem to understand," he said. "You will not be writing your speech. It is the
Premier's prerogative to write the speeches made on opening
day by the mover and seconder of the Address in Reply."

I thanked Smallwood for offering to write my speech.
"But with everything else you have on your mind, with the
House opening and all," I said, "I will save you the trouble—I
will write my own speech." He suddenly became very irritable
and, in a tone of voice that told me he was in no mood to

argue, he said, "Drop in here on Wednesday morning and pick up your speech—it will be ready for you."

I told him, "I am sorry, but if I cannot write my own speech, I will have to decline your offer to move the Address in Reply. I find it difficult to read a speech written by another person."

Because Smallwood had already announced publicly that I would be moving the Address in Reply, I realized that in the final analysis he would have to give in. Obviously, that thought had not escaped him either. He called me "a damn independent Bonavista bayman." As I was leaving his office, he called me back and said sarcastically, "Mr. Carter, would it be asking too much for you to let me see your speech before you go to the House of Assembly on Wednesday afternoon? In case you have forgotten, I am still the Premier of this Province, you know."

I assured him that I would be pleased to "run it by him" before I delivered it in the House of Assembly.

On Wednesday morning I went to Smallwood's office with the text of my speech. As I entered, Steve Neary (who was seconding the Address in Reply) was leaving, his speech neatly stapled together and ready to be read that afternoon. Smallwood made it a point of telling me that he had written Neary's speech. I handed Smallwood a copy of my speech, which he read without saying a word. I expected him to insist on several changes, if for no other reason than to prove a point. But he didn't.

He carefully read every word, after which he said, "It contains one glaring mistake. Throughout the speech, you keep saying the Government *is* going to do this, and the Government *is* going to do that—as if the Government consisted of one individual. If you were referring to the Government of the Soviet Union, where they have a dictatorship, or some Banana Republic in South America, you would be right. But don't ever forget that under our democratic

177

system, governments are made up of a number of individuals acting as a group and, in that context, the word government is a collective noun."

As if he knew what I was thinking, he stared at me for a while and, with a sly grin on his face, handed me back my speech. "An excellent job," he said. "However, don't forget what I told you. In a democracy like ours, it is more appropriate that the word government be construed as a plural, collective noun. I am sure you do not want to convey the impression that we have a one-man dictatorship in Newfoundland, now do you?"

Twenty-five

Meeting the President

Newfoundland politics is the kind of activity from which one needs a break now and then. In 1964, Muriel and I went on a short vacation in Florida. On our way back to St. John's, we decided to stop over in Washington, DC for a couple of days to visit various historic sites, including the grave of the late President John F. Kennedy in Mount Arlington Cemetery.

Arriving at Dulles International Airport on Sunday evening, we were surprised to learn that our Canadian money was worthless. With fifty cents in American currency, we were stranded in a strange city and unable to get the things you normally require in such circumstances. In those days, there were no banking machines or other means of obtaining instant cash or credit, especially on a Sunday evening in a foreign country.

We managed to get a ride in a courtesy vehicle to a nearby motel, where we spent the night. By the time we had checked in and freshened up, both of us were hungry and in the mood for dinner. We telephoned the desk to make reservations for a table in the dining room, only to learn that except for the usual soft drink and junk food dispensers, there was no place in the establishment to buy a meal. So, until we could drive to a Washington bank in the morning and arrange for some American money, we would have to survive on a Coke and a bag of potato chips each.

There were no banks within walking distance of our motel, which was located close to the airport. Washington was twenty miles away, across the Potomac River. The next morning I arranged for a taxi to take us to a bank in Washington. I explained our situation to the driver; he agreed to wait while we conducted our banking business, then drive us back to the motel.

I have forgotten the name of the bank—I believe it was the Riggs National Bank of Washington. I recall that it was situated on or near Pennsylvania Avenue, in the general area of the White House and other well known historic buildings and landmarks. As we entered the bank, the receptionist arranged for us to meet the foreign exchange manager, a middle-aged Englishman with the appearance and mannerisms of the stereotypical English butler, very polite and patronizing, the sort of character that frequently appears in British movies.

Inviting us into his office, he immediately started the process of clearing my personal cheque, which was drawn on a St. John's branch of the Bank of Nova Scotia. In those days, it was no simple matter to walk into an American bank and cash a cheque drawn on a Canadian bank. I had to provide proof of my identity, following which a telephone call had to be placed to my bank in St. John's to have the cheque certified. Since I was travelling without a passport, the identification cards I produced, including a birth certificate, didn't have my picture on them, which further complicated the process.

In those days, there was no such thing as direct dialling. Long distance calls had to go through an operator, which frequently took time to arrange, especially on Monday mornings when line traffic was heavy. I offered to wait in the outer office until the manager was ready to complete the transaction. However, he appeared to be in no hurry to get rid of us. In fact, he insisted that we sit in his office until the call came through. He was obviously enjoying our discussion, most of which centred around American politics and life in Washington during the Kennedy era.

Trying desperately to make conversation, I told him that my wife and I were great admirers of their President and were anxious to meet him during our stay in Washington. "Perhaps we could have a picture taken shaking his hand," I said.

"That shouldn't be a problem," he said. "Our President is noted for being quite accessible, especially to Canadians." With that, he reached for his telephone and told his secretary to get the President's executive assistant on the line.

A few seconds later, he spoke to the man on the phone, "I say, old chap, I have with me in my office two charming people who are visiting here from Canada. They are great admirers of our President, and their fondest wish is to have an opportunity to meet him while they are in Washington. They just want to shake his hand and, if it is all right with the President, have a picture taken with him."

Placing his hand over the mouthpiece, he looked our way and whispered, "He's having a word with the President now to see when he will see you." Moments later, I heard him say, "That's splendid, old chap. We'll be over shortly." With that, he hung up the telephone.

Before the manager had a chance to say anything, his secretary poked her head around the door and called him out to take the call from my bank that had come through while he was making arrangements for us to meet the President.

I said to Muriel, "I want a picture taken with President Johnson and, if possible, I'll take one of you talking with the first lady." I gave Muriel a crash course in photography and arranged the settings on the camera, in readiness for the big event.

Most of my adult life has revolved around politics and politicians. While other tourists were collecting autographed pictures of movie stars and well known athletes, I never missed an opportunity to have pictures taken with political leaders and heads of state. My collection of pictures taken with famous personalities includes German Chancellor Willy Brandt, President Tito of Yugoslavia, President Richard Nixon, the President of Cyprus, Archbishop Marcarius, the President of Iceland, every Prime Minister of Canada since Mackenzie King, and a group picture taken with Queen Elizabeth and Prince Charles.

While Lyndon Johnson was not one of my favourite American Presidents, he was a world leader; I welcomed the opportunity to have a picture taken with him and Mrs. Johnson.

Within minutes, the foreign exchange manager returned with my money. He then put on his jacket, straightened his necktie, and said, "Okay, old chap, let's go. It's all arranged—you and your good wife are going to get your wish, we're off to meet the President."

I told him how surprised we were that he could arrange for us to meet the President on such short notice. I said, "You amaze me. You must be a man of considerable influence in Washington. I never dreamed that it would be so easy to meet your President. I have heard of cases where people have had to wait for months to even get close to such an important person, much less meet him." I made him promise me that, if he ever visited Newfoundland, he would let us show him around and perhaps introduce him to Premier Joey Smallwood.

I could tell by the way the manager was acting that he was not averse to flattery. He literally strutted out through the bank's general office into the main foyer. I told him that we had a taxi waiting for us near the front entrance. I suggested, "Rather than putting you through the trouble of getting your car, we could use the taxi."

He assured me that it was unnecessary, adding, "We'll walk to his office."

He led us past the bank's main entrance leading to the

street where my taxi was waiting, and headed towards the elevator. Suddenly, I knew that things were not what they appeared to be. Directing us into the elevator, he pressed a button indicating the tenth floor. Still unsure what was happening, we followed him down a long corridor to a door marked JAMES B. McGIVEN, PRESIDENT. I knew then that the foreign exchange manager was under the impression from the start that we wanted to meet the President of the *bank*, not the President of the *United States of America*!

We were ushered into the Bank President's walnut-paneled office where an elderly man in a three-piece, pin-striped suit welcomed us with such enthusiasm you would think we were long-lost brothers. I tried to act normally as I went through the charade of pretending to have had a lifelong dream realized: meeting the Bank President. The foreign exchange manager introduced us, then told the President how anxious we were to shake his hand and maybe have a picture taken with him. After posing for several pictures, including one with the foreign exchange manager, we chatted for a few minutes over a cup of coffee.

As we were preparing to leave, I thanked the Bank President for making it possible for my wife and me to meet him. "I have to commend you," I said, "on your choice of a foreign exchange manager. In all my travels, I've never met his likes. You should be very proud of him."

As we were standing around waiting for the elevator, the foreign exchange manager was beaming. He said, "I can't tell you, old chap, how much I appreciate what you said to the President. I can't tell you how much I needed that lift this morning. What a simply jolly way to start a week!"

On our way back to the motel, Muriel commented that I had put on a stellar performance. "A Broadway actor could not have done it any better; it was an Oscar-winning performance." she said.

I reminded her that the Bank President was no slouch, either, when it came to putting on an act.

Welcome to Ottawa

Twenty-six

The '68 Election

The results of the 1968 federal election started to trickle in a few minutes after the polls closed. With Conservative Jim McGrath already declared the winner in St. John's East, the pandemonium that was on the verge of breaking out at my headquarters all evening finally erupted. The Canadian Press had declared me the winner in St. John's West. Hundreds of enthusiastic supporters from all parts of the riding descended on my campaign headquarters in the basement of the old Pentecostal Tabernacle on Casey Street to join in the celebration. The Conservatives in St. John's West had waited fifteen years for this victory. The last federal election victory they had celebrated was in 1953, when William J. Browne defeated Liberal Leonard Miller.

The cheering that began soon after the first returns came in continued as Canadian Press conceded other seats in Atlantic Canada to the Conservatives. With the Conservatives leading in six of the seven Newfoundland seats, it soon became obvious that Don Jamieson would be the only Liberal incumbent to survive. The Conservative show of strength in Atlantic Canada, particulary in the Liberal bastion of Newfoundland, buoyed the spirits of Conservatives right across Canada. That is, until the returns started coming in from the central provinces, showing a heavy trend towards the Liberals.

By the time I arrived at the campaign headquarters with my family, traffic was at a standstill and the area was crowded with well-wishers. The policemen—who were there trying to keep the traffic moving—had to assist us as we tried to enter the building. Before I knew what was happening, I found myself on the shoulders of two burly supporters, being carried towards the platform as a cheering crowd shoved their way along with us. I spoke briefly to the crowd, thanking them for their support, and proceeded to celebrate with the others. Muriel and I had to leave at 10:30 to meet Party Leader Gerald Ottenheimer and other party officials at Hotel Newfoundland, where they were holding a press conference to comment on the election results and to congratulate the newly elected Members of Parliament for St. John's East and West. When we arrived back at campaign headquarters an hour later, it was even more crowded than when we had left.

Dewey Fitzgerald, a well known St. John's character who worked on my campaign, suddenly got the urge to pay a personal visit to my Liberal opponent's campaign headquarters in the Laurier Club on Hamilton Avenue. He wanted to see firsthand how Richard Cashin and his workers were taking defeat. Since Dewey was a known supporter of mine, the welcome he received was somewhat less than cordial. Before he got a chance to enter the building, one of Cashin's workers met him at the front door and demanded to know what he wanted.

Not noted for being timid or tactful, Dewey did not take kindly to being shouted at. Forcing his way into the Club's reception area, he entered the room where a number of well known Liberals were sitting around, trying to figure out what had gone wrong. He was immediately ordered off the premises.

"What are you doing here, anyway?" one of them shouted. "Why aren't you down celebrating with your buddy, Walter Carter?" In his best St. John's Irish brogue, Dewey shouted back, "Go shag yourself. There's no law against goin' to a wake, is there?" With that, he unceremoniously left the premises, bobbing and weaving as he frantically tried to dodge the empty beer bottles that suddenly started coming at him from all directions.

Prior to the 1968 election, St. John's West had a reputation for being the most unstable federal riding in Newfoundland. It changed political hands five times in seven elections. Its political history as a federal constituency officially began on June 27, 1949, when Progressive Conservative William J. Browne received a 1,516-vote majority over his Liberal opponent, Gregory Power. But victory was short-lived for Browne and the Conservatives. In the 1953 general election, Liberal candidate James Power won the seat with a 940-vote margin over Browne.

The next flip-flop came in 1957, when the Diefenbaker Conservatives won a minority government. Browne turned the tables on incumbent James Power and won with a majority of 2,090 votes. In the next election in 1958, Browne gained the largest margin of victory in the ridings' history when he defeated his nearest opponent by 5,615 votes.

The tide turned again in 1962, when Liberal newcomer Richard Cashin beat the veteran Browne by a slim margin of 24 votes. Browne protested the results, charging election irregularities, and the election was finally declared void. Consequently, St. John's West was without a Member in the House of Commons until the general election of 1963. In that election, Richard Cashin confirmed the victory he thought he had in 1962, this time with a decisive 3,727-vote margin. In the 1965 general election, Cashin easily retained his seat and increased his margin of victory by defeating three opponents, Progressive Conservative Gerald Ottenheimer, Esau Thoms of the New Democratic Party, and Cary Skinner of the Social Credit Party. Cashin received 4,427 votes over his nearest opponent, Gerald Ottenheimer, who subsequently became the Leader of the provincial Conservative Party.

I won the federal riding of St. John's West three times for the Conservative Party while it was under Robert Stanfield's leadership. In 1968, I won it by a margin of 4,700 votes; in 1972, by a 6,000-vote margin; and in 1974, by a 8,500-vote margin.

I became a supporter of the federal Progressive Conservative Party when Robert Stanfield was elected leader in 1967. Shortly after the 1968 federal election was called, I was approached by several Conservative Party supporters, including well known party workers Ern Antle and Jim Crane, who wanted me to seek the nomination in St. John's West. Since Antle and Crane were close to the provincial party leader, I had reason to believe that while Ottenheimer's position prevented him from publicly endorsing my candidacy, he and other high-ranking Conservatives were anxious that I become their candidate.

Although I avoided saying anything in public that would cause the media to speculate on why I was no longer actively involved with the Liberal Party, the hierarchy of the Conservative Party were aware of the differences that existed between myself and Joe Smallwood.

My disaffection with the Liberal Party came to a head in the fall of 1965, while I was still a member of the House of Assembly for White Bay North. I discovered that wearing two hats—as a city councillor and a member of the Liberal caucus—was extremely difficult. Frequently, those of us who were in that position found ourselves in the untenable stance of having to defend the concerns of the St. John's council against the government and the rest of the Liberal caucus, most of whom represented rural districts and were less than sympathetic to the needs of the capital city.

It also placed Smallwood in a difficult position. It soon became obvious to him that he could not count on our support if a disagreement arose between the council and his government, which frequently happened. He was not used to having members of his caucus exhibit that kind of independence. Bill Adams' announcement in the summer of

1965—that he intended to resign his seat in the Legislature and run for mayor of St. John's—was the proverbial last straw. Smallwood could not understand why anybody would walk away from a seat in the House of Assembly to become mayor of St. John's.

In an earlier chapter, I related that Smallwood wanted me to resign my seat in White Bay North to run in St. John's West in a by-election to fill the vacancy created by Bill Adams' resignation. My refusal to accept Smallwood's offer, which he interpreted as turning my back on him and the Liberal Party, soured our relationship.

A few weeks after that incident, Smallwood invited me to his office for a chat. It seems that word had gotten back to him that I was disenchanted with the Liberal Party and somewhat less than supportive of some of its policies.

Obviously, he was a firm believer in the old axiom, "The best defence is a good offence." As soon as I sat down, Smallwood went on the attack. "What has gotten into you?" he began. "I gave you a job in my office. I took you by the hand and got you elected in White Bay North. And now, I hear that you are ready to kick over the traces." Before I could respond, he fired another round. "I have it from a reliable source that you will vote against the government when we introduce legislation in the fall sitting of the House to put Newfoundland on the Atlantic Provinces time zone."

Under no circumstances would I support any such legislation, since I knew it was being done solely for the benefit of certain people in the broadcasting business who wanted to bring their local program scheduling in line with the other Atlantic Provinces. In my view, changing Newfoundland's unique time zone for that reason was not justified, since it would deprive us of half an hour of daylight in the evenings, which we could ill afford to lose, especially in the late fall and winter when it is dark by four o'clock in the afternoon. During those months our children would be walking home from school in darkness.

I discussed the proposed time-change legislation with my old friend Max Lane, the Minister of Fisheries. I told him I would not support such legislation. I knew that as a Cabinet Minister, Max would have to make the Premier aware of my comments, which he obviously did. Within a couple of days, Captain Uriah Strickland, the Party whip, let it be known that there would not be a free vote on the legislation. Members of the Liberal caucus were expected to support the government.

Strickland did not mince words. He said, "The Skipper is adamant. Those of you who choose to do otherwise might as well pick up your seats, march across the floor of the House, and plant them down with the Tory Opposition, because you will no longer be permitted to sit as a Liberal."

I am still not sure what happened, but that was the last we heard of the time-change legislation. Obviously, Smallwood had sensed trouble and decided to allow it to die on the order paper.

Becoming angrier by the minute and still giving me no chance to say a word, Smallwood continued his attack, "You are being influenced by Harry Mews and that bunch of St. John's Tories at City Hall."

Convinced by this time that he had frightened me half to death, Smallwood continued to give me hell. He told me I should have better sense than to waste my time piddling around with trivial things like potholes, garbage collection and the like, when there were other, more important issues that should be receiving my attention.

I sat for fifteen or twenty minutes, trying hard to act nonchalantly as Smallwood worked himself into a rage. "You have to make up your mind within a couple of days what you want to do," he said. "You must decide which side your bread is buttered on. Do you want to remain a member of the Liberal caucus where you have a bright future, or carry on as a city councillor where you will continue to be up to your backside in potholes, sewage and household garbage?"

I thanked him for his concern for my future. At the same time, I assured him I would not require two or three days to give him my answer—he could have it now.

With that, he walked over to where I was sitting and gave me a pat on the back. "I knew you would make the right decision," he said. "You are showing a lot of good sense.

"Now that we have that settled," he continued, "I am sure we both agree that it will serve no useful purpose for anything we discussed here today to appear in the newspapers. However, in case it does get out, you should head it off by making a statement tomorrow morning stating that you will not be running in the fall municipal election. You will be devoting all your time to provincial politics. You should also make it clear that you continue to be supportive of the Liberal Party and will seek re-election in White Bay North in the next general election."

When I finally got a chance to speak, I told Smallwood that he had obviously made an assumption that he had no right to make. I reminded him that I had *not* said I wouldn't seek re-election to city council. "In fact," I said, "it's the other way around. I will be running for council when the time comes, but I will not be seeking a second term as a Liberal in White Bay North."

Before he got a chance to go on the attack again, I told him I wanted an opportunity to speak. "And, you have a choice," I added. "Do you want to hear firsthand what I have to say, or would you prefer to read it in *The Evening Telegram*?"

He did not say anything but motioned with his hands for me to continue.

I told Smallwood essentially what I have repeated many times in the past thirty years. I had no reason to question his personal honesty or integrity. His judgement, yes. I told him that I could not say the same for some of the people around him. Smallwood's problem was that he trusted everybody implicitly. Consequently, he was easy pickings for many shysters and charlatans. The leeches in whom he placed his trust, including certain local businessmen whose names remain household words in this province, devised and executed their cosy cost-plus and leaseback schemes, on which they amassed fortunes at the expense of Newfoundland taxpayers and, in the process, Smallwood's reputation. These were the real culprits, not Smallwood.

By this time I knew there was no turning back. With the preamble over, I decided to get it all off my chest. I told Smallwood that I was not prepared to continue supporting certain policies of his administration. "You have allowed yourself to be taken over by certain corrupt business interests who are fleecing the people of this province and who, in the process, have made it difficult for anybody with an ounce of guts or independence to remain in the Liberal caucus." I told him that in my view it was guilt by association. "You are being lumped in with these individuals and, while I do not necessarily agree, you and your administration are being perceived by average Newfoundlanders as being corrupt."

Smallwood leaped from his chair and started walking back and forth, unable to control his anger. "How dare you make such an accusation?" he shouted. "Name one thing that we have done that would justify that kind of a comment from you. I challenge you. Give me one example where we have acted improperly."

Trying my best to remain calm, I told him that I could identify numerous incidents in which certain companies and individuals were fleecing the government and people of the province. "And what's even worse," I said, "is that they seem to be doing it with your blessing."

Realizing that I meant business, Smallwood regained his composure, sat back in his chair, and listened attentively.

When I finished, he paused, got out of his chair and slowly walked over to where I was sitting. I will never know what was going through his mind at that moment, but he sombrely shook my hand and wished me well. That was the last time we spoke to each other for ten years.

Despite our differences, I was convinced then—and I remain convinced—that Smallwood left politics in the early 1970s with little more personal wealth than he had when he first entered politics. While I have never presumed to have been his close personal confidant, the eight years that I worked in his office in the 1950s gave me an opportunity to observe the real Joe Smallwood and to get to know him better than most people, including some of his former colleagues and beneficiaries who, for questionable reasons, continue to take it upon themselves to be his judge, jury and executioner. Mark Twain said, "If you befriend and feed a starving dog, it will not bite you. That is the principal difference between a dog and a man."

People who were close to Smallwood know that he showed absolutely no interest in accumulating money or personal possessions. During the many times he invited me to his St. John's apartment for a chat after he retired, I saw nothing to indicate that his attitude in that respect had changed or that his personal financial position had improved. Unfortunately, I am unable to say the same for some of the people that Smallwood had around him in his years in power.

Neither our meeting that afternoon, nor what transpired between us, was ever reported in the news media. I sought re-election to City Council in 1965 and was returned with a substantially increased majority. When a provincial election was called a few months later, I issued a terse, one-paragraph statement to the effect that I would not seek re-election and left it at that. When Deputy Mayor John Crosbie resigned in 1966 to enter provincial politics, I replaced him and re-

mained in that position until August 1968 when I went to
Ottawa to take my seat in the House of Commons.

My decision to seek the Conservative Party's nomination
in St. John's West was not made lightly. It involved many
hours of discussion with Muriel, our children, and some of my
close friends. Since I chose not to say anything to the news
media about my break with Smallwood and the Liberal Party,
supporters of the Conservative Party in St. John's West were
unaware of it. Many of them viewed my candidacy for the
Party's nomination with some scepticism.

Jack McDonald, a highly respected farmer in Kilbride
and a lifelong Conservative, was understandably sceptical
when I visited him looking for his support. Without beating
around the bush, he said, "Walter, I was always under the
impression that you were a Liberal. I want to know one thing
before I promise to support you. Did Joey Smallwood put you
up to running in St. John's West to split the vote and elect
Cashin?"

I assured Jack that he had nothing to fear; I was running
to defeat Richard Cashin, not to help him get elected.

Jack was relieved. We shook hands and, from that moment on, he was not only my most ardent supporter, he also
became one of my best friends.

Jack McDonald's scepticism, and that of other Conservatives in St. John's West, was not without justification. In an
earlier federal election campaign in which William J. Browne
was the Conservative candidate, a last minute entry into the
race was one William Joseph Bowe, a completely unknown St.
John's resident who, minutes before nominations closed,
showed up at the office of the Chief Electoral Officer and
announced his intention to run for the Social Credit Party in
St. John's West. For obvious reasons, William Joseph Bowe's
entry into the St. John's West campaign caused the Conservative Party and the candidate great concern. The name of
William Joseph Bowe on a ballot with that of William Joseph

Browne, in that order, would undoubtedly cause confusion. In a tight race, it could conceivably cost Browne the election. It did not take Jack McDonald and his fellows Conservatives long to smell a rat. Bowe's last minute candidacy was engineered by certain well known Liberals in St. John's West who wanted to confuse the electorate.

There was a collective sigh of relief within the Conservative Party and Browne's campaign organization when it was discovered a few days later that William J. Bowe did not meet the age requirement to be a federal candidate. He was under 21. It was also discovered that he fraudulently gave his name as William Joseph Bowe: according to his birth certificate he was William Jerome Bowe.

While I have been criticized by some for changing political parties, I can never be accused of opportunism. I have never crossed the floor of the Legislature or switched parties between elections. When I walked away from the Liberal Party in 1966, and subsequently became a Conservative candidate in the 1968 federal election, the political fortunes of the provincial and federal Conservative Parties were at an all-time low. Most political observers were predicting that Pierre Elliott Trudeau, the forty-eight-year-old swinging phenomenon who came out of nowhere, would sweep the country. In Newfoundland, where all seven of our Members of Parliament and all but three of the forty-two members of the House of Assembly were Liberals, the prospects for a Conservative win were dismal.

With the meeting to select a candidate for the June 25 election tentatively planned for May 1, the people who were encouraging me to run were pressing me for a decision. They would need a few days to drum up support for my candidacy, especially in the rural areas of the riding where support appeared to be very strong. It was agreed that I would contact the Party leader, Gerald Ottenheimer, by ten o'clock on Friday night and give him my answer. The St. John's *Evening*

Telegram had already speculated that I would seek the nomination.

Robert Stanfield's election in 1967 as leader of the Progressive Conservative Party had already convinced me to vote for the Conservatives. However, as the deadline approached, I was far from convinced that I was ready to go all the way. Voting for the Conservatives was one thing, but contesting the election as a Conservative candidate was another matter. By eight o'clock on Friday evening, my mind was made up; I would telephone Gerald Ottenheimer and advise him that I would not be a candidate.

Before I had a chance to make the call to Ottenheimer, the telephone rang and a somewhat slurred voice on the other end wanted to know if there was any truth to the story in that day's *Telegram* that I was considering running for the Conservative Party against Richard Cashin in St. John's West.

Since I considered it only fair that Ottenheimer should be the first to be hear of my decision, I was not about to bare my soul to the telephone stranger, except to caution him that he should not believe everything he read in the newspapers.

Taking that to mean there was no truth to the story, the caller then congratulated me for having made a very wise decision. Not content to leave it at that, he became belligerent, almost to the point of daring me to run. "What a slaughtering it would have been had you decided to take on Cashin," he said. "You would have been devoured." Still not content to leave well enough alone, he proceeded to tell me what a fool I was to even think about running against Richard Cashin. "You, a Bonavista bayman, and a Protestant at that," he said, "thinking you could defeat a Cashin in St. John's West!"

I have since wondered how different my life might have been were it not for that phone call, or had the caller the good sense to know when to hang up. In that instant I reversed my earlier decision, then and there deciding to seek the Conservative nomination in St. John's West.

I allowed the conversation to continue for a couple more minutes. Then I interrupted the caller and said deliberately, "You have obviously put the wrong interpretation on my answer to your first question. I did not say I would not be running; I merely suggested that you should not believe everything you read in the newspapers."

After a long pause, the voice on the other end said, "What do you mean by that—are you running or not?" I said, "I meant just that—you should not believe everything you read in the newspapers. The *Telegram* article you referred to said I might be running. I expect the matter will be put to rest in tomorrow's paper. I am not sure you will like what you see, but I suggest that you read it anyway."

Obviously surprised, the caller paused for a few seconds, as if trying to figure out what I was trying to tell him. Then, as if he suddenly got the message, he unleashed some of the most abusive language I have ever heard.

I visited Gerald Ottenheimer later that evening at his home on Waterford Bridge Road and informed him I would be honoured to run in St. John's West, if the Conservatives chose me as their candidate. Ottenheimer then contacted the executive of the St. John's West Constituency Association and suggested that the nomination meeting be held Monday evening. With two other candidates to choose from, the five hundred Conservatives who crowded into Canon Sterling Auditorium on that Monday evening elected me as their candidate on the first ballot.

The next day, I received a telegram from the Honourable William J. Browne, who was then living in Ottawa, offering his congratulations and best wishes. He said he would be pleased to return to St. John's the following day and remain there during the campaign to give me the benefit of his experience as a former Member of the House of Commons for St. John's

West. Naturally, I accepted his offer and, within a couple of days, he and I were sitting in my home with Ank Murphy and other well known St. John's Conservatives, planning the campaign.

As a newcomer to the Conservative Party, I was pleasantly surprised by the manner in which Browne and other long-time St. John's Conservatives accepted me into the fold. There were other reasons why their support meant much to me. Known as a Roman Catholic riding, St. John's West was evenly split between urban and rural. Half the voters were in St. John's and Mount Pearl; the other half were in rural communities on the Southern Shore, the Cape Shore, St. Mary's Bay and Placentia Bay, where at least 95 percent of the people were Roman Catholic. It was important that prominent Roman Catholics like Browne be seen to be actively supporting my candidacy.

With the help of my old friends Jim Crane and Ern Antle, things started to move within hours after I won the nomination. Despite the apparent absence of any kind of grassroots Conservative organization in the riding, key party workers throughout the riding (including Placentia East, St. Mary's Bay and Ferryland) were in touch with me, offering to support my candidacy. Long-time Conservatives Bill Patterson in Placentia, Ray McDonald in Salmonier, and Mike Ryan in Bay Bulls were my biggest supporters in their respective districts. They worked like Trojans to help me win not only that campaign but subsequent campaigns, all of which I won with increased majorities.

One of the most important spin-off benefits I derived from the 1968 federal election campaign was the opportunity it gave me to meet some of the finest, most genuine people in this province, including the three gentlemen noted above. I have nothing but fond memories of my association with the riding and the people of St. John's West, particularly the people who worked on my campaigns.

The Carter family in 1968.

Before the 1968 election, it was widely believed that a candidate's religious affiliation was an important factor in both of the St. John's seats. It would be pointless, said the pundits, to run a Protestant in a predominantly Roman Catholic riding and expect to win. Conversely, they were convinced that Roman Catholic candidates would find it equally difficult to get elected in districts where Protestants were in the majority.

I take considerable pride in the fact that I proved the pundits wrong. I won five elections, three federal and two provincial, in ridings in which Roman Catholics were in the majority. It was impossible to determine if religion was a factor in the urban parts of the riding because of the density of the population and the number of polls. However, it was relatively simple in the rural communities. The only polls I lost were in communities where Protestants were in the majority; in the communities where the entire population was Catholic, I won every poll.

My two provincial election victories in the all-Catholic provincial district of St. Mary's-the-Capes are also a source of considerable satisfaction for me. I again proved the pundits wrong. My friend Christopher Pratt and his wife Mary were—as far as I knew—the only non-Catholics in St. Mary's-the-Capes. He telephoned me during one campaign, assuring me that I had no worries. I would get 100% of the Protestant votes in the district.

The St. John's *Evening Telegram* of June 26, 1968 noted, "The Carter victory in the federal riding of St. John's West marks two firsts in Newfoundland politics. He is the first Protestant (Anglican) to be elected in St. John's West and he is the first Liberal Member of the House of Assembly to have bolted the party and won a subsequent election."

With the election over and the excitement of election night now just a memory, my wife and I had important decisions to make. Establishing a residence in Ottawa with eight school-age children would not be a simple matter. After many family discussions and with practically no adverse reaction from our children, we decided to move lock, stock and barrel to Ottawa—and to endeavour to be there and settled away in time for the beginning of the new school year. Fortunately, we had two months in which to execute our plans.

With all our household effects packed and ready to be shipped the same day, the ten of us left St. John's in the family station wagon on August 24 and headed to Argentia, where we boarded the ferry that would take us to North Sydney, the first leg of our 3000-mile journey to the nation's capital.

Keeping track of eight children is difficult at the best of times. But trying to keep track of them onboard an ocean-going ferry for eighteen hours is something else. They were all

Being sworn in as a Member of Parliment for St. John's West following the 1968 election. Seated is John Lundrigan. Standing from left to right: Jim McGrath; Walter Carter; Alister Fraser, Clerk of Commons.

over the place. Our eldest daughter, Donna Lynn, helped keep track of her younger sisters, Bonnie and Susan; Roger, our eldest son, helped us keep track of his younger brothers, David, Paul, Glenn and Gregory. The boys were much more adventuresome and difficult to control than the girls, who contented themselves playing with their dolls and the games we brought along for their amusement. Our sons were contented only when they were climbing something or hanging over the vessel's rails. When they were not exploring the vessel, they were in the ship's cafeteria, where they spent a disproportionate amount of the allowances we gave them for the entire trip.

We arrived in North Sydney early the next day and lost no time beginning the next leg of our journey to Ottawa. With ten people and hundreds of pounds of personal effects crammed into our 1965 Buick station wagon, including the items strapped to the roof rack, the vehicle's undercarriage was almost scraping the ground.

Our first day of highway travel could hardly be characterized as smooth. We limped into Truro that afternoon with our tailpipe hanging off, a punctured gas tank and a flat tire. When the mechanic put the station wagon on the ramp to install a new tailpipe, we were both horror-stricken. Gasoline was dripping from the punctured gas tank, within inches of where the damaged tailpipe had been scraping the surface of the road, sending sparks flying in all directions each time we hit a bump.

"It was a miracle," said the mechanic, "that you were not all blown to kingdom come."

I was glad that Muriel and our children were not within hearing distance of the mechanic as he went into all the gory details of what could have happened.

By four o'clock we were ready to get on the road again. That night we reached New Brunswick, where we had difficulty finding a motel with enough rooms available to accommodate the ten of us. By ten o'clock, we were ready to call it a day. We decided to take the next place we found, even if it meant all of us would have to share the same room. And that is precisely what we had to do. In a small motel a few miles east of Moncton, our entire family spent the night in one room. We ate chicken and chips, watched television and, in some of the strangest positions imaginable, fell asleep.

The remainder of our trip to Ottawa went reasonably well, except for a couple more flat tires and the occasional outbreak of hostilities between the children in the rear seat. We made it to Ottawa in one piece. As we approached the city of Ottawa, we came upon a sign that read, "Welcome to Ottawa. Population 225,000."

Oblivious to the attention I was attracting from passing motorists, I pulled up by the sign and, with a black marker, ceremoniously altered the sign to read, "Welcome to Ottawa. Population 225,0*10*."

Twenty-seven

Nuclear Weapons in Argentia

On June 11, 1970 I asked a question in the House of Commons that sent shockwaves through the United States Defence Department and created a serious rift in Canada/US relations. At least that was the way it was characterized at the time by Mitchell Sharp, Canada's Secretary of State for External Affairs, when he discussed it with me outside the Commons Chamber. He also accused me of breaching one of the most closely guarded secrets of the North-American Aerospace Defence Command during the Cold War.

If you were around in the 1940s or 1950s, chances are you spent a fair amount of time thinking, or at least being bombarded with information and rhetoric, about nuclear weapons. After World War Two, a new age of military strategy prevailed. The United States and the Soviet Union accumulated massive arsenals of nuclear weapons and developed elaborate systems of delivery and defence. One of the best-kept secrets in Newfoundland, perhaps in Canada, during the late 1960s and early 1970s was that the Americans were stockpiling a significant part of their nuclear weapons arsenal at their naval base in Argentia.

I gave an undertaking to the person who gave me the information that under no circumstances would I reveal his identity. And I intend to honour that undertaking. Consequently, I will withhold the name of my informant and that of the other person involved. Suffice it to say that one was a Member of Parliament, and the other a senior naval officer.

Over a drink one evening in Halifax with a friend who was

a high-ranking naval officer, my colleague learned that, with the full knowledge and consent of the Government of Canada, the Americans were storing nuclear weapons in Argentia, Newfoundland, as part of a North Atlantic defence strategy. Since Argentia was in my federal riding, my colleague felt that I should be aware of this situation. He also felt that I should take the Government of Canada to task for exposing the people in the Argentia area, and Newfoundlanders generally, to the dangers of having nuclear weapons stored in their midst.

The very thought of nuclear weapons capable of awesome destruction being stored in a densely populated Newfoundland community, surrounded by tens of thousands of innocent people, was frightening, to say the least. Since I had absolutely no reason to question the authenticity of the information I had received, or the credibility of its source, I was convinced I had a responsibility to air it publicly; my constituents, indeed every Newfoundlander, had a right to know what was going on.

An important part of the proceedings of the House of Commons is the daily Question Period. Shown on the order paper as "Oral Questions," it is 45 minutes in which Opposition Members, and sometimes Members of the governing Party, are given the opportunity to question the Prime Minister or his Ministers.

A few minutes after the House of Commons convened on June 11, 1970, I sent a note to the Speaker, asking him to recognize me during Question Period; I had a question of considerable urgency for the Secretary of State for External Affairs.

About halfway through Question Period, the Speaker looked my way and called the name of my riding, which meant I should proceed. Because of the time constraint, questions must be brief, to the point, and concern a matter of some urgency. Usually, the Speaker permits a short preamble to the first question. However, when asking a follow-up question, one must get to the point immediately or risk being called to order by the Speaker.

In the preamble to my first question, I told the Speaker that I wanted to question the Secretary of State for External Affairs, Mitchell Sharp, on an urgent matter. I said, "It concerns the stockpiling of nuclear weapons in Newfoundland, more specifically, in Argentia, which is part of the riding I represent. Mr. Speaker, it has come to my attention that nuclear weapons are currently being stockpiled at the United Stated Naval Base in Argentia. I want to know from the Minister if the United States Government requested permission from the Government of Canada to stockpile nuclear weapons in Newfoundland. If so, on what date was permission given, by whom was it given, and was the Government of Newfoundland consulted or made aware of the situation in that regard?"

I kept looking directly at Mitchell Sharp as I asked my question. The moment I finished the preamble, I knew that something was wrong. Sharp looked as if he had just seen a ghost. He hesitated for a few seconds before he stood to respond, nervously exchanging glances with the Prime Minister. While a Minister is not compelled to answer a question, if the question is in order and concerns a matter of some urgency, there is an unwritten rule which says he is expected to provide an answer. Sharp seemed to be in a quandary. Would he respond to my question, or would he take a chance on ignoring it? He was obviously weighing the odds; it was clearly a case of being damned if he did, and damned if he didn't. Finally, trying his best to act nonchalantly, he said, "Mr. Speaker, I have had to answer questions of this kind on many occasions by saying that I can make no comment on the positioning of nuclear weapons in Canada, either to comment negatively or positively."

Sharp's response, and the manner in which he replied,

convinced me that my question had been right on target; nuclear weapons were in fact being stockpiled in Argentia by the United States Government. Obviously, it caused the Minister and the Prime Minister considerable discomfort and embarrassment. However, I was not about to let them off the hook; they would have to account for their actions. I believed that exposing the people of the Argentia area to the most destructive weapon known to the human race should not be taken lightly.

I then asked the Minister a supplementary question, "Mr. Speaker, while I acknowledge the fact that my question to the Minister has placed him and the government in a difficult position, surely he must appreciate the difficult position in which he and his government have placed the people of Newfoundland. Therefore, would he and the Prime Minister now tell the people of Newfoundland, whose lives they have placed in jeopardy, precisely where they stand? If an explosion were to occur in the Argentia area, what should they do? Should they start praying, or should they start running?"

Sharp's response was terse and to the point, and again he tried to act nonchalantly. He said, "Mr. Speaker, I think the reason for not discussing these matters is fairly obvious; it is one of security."

When Question Period was over, Sharp motioned for me to meet him outside in the foyer. Trying his best to control his anger, he told me that my question would have serious repercussions in Washington and would jeopardize the entire American military strategy for the defence of North America. He said the deployment of nuclear weapons on the North American continent was a closely guarded secret. Neither the American nor the Canadian government wanted to alert the Russians that nuclear weapons were being kept in a state of readiness and stockpiled on Canadian soil. "The Americans," he said, "will never again trust the Government of Canada. Your question this afternoon will not only undermine the entire US defence strategy, but it will set Canada/US relations back to where they were in the Diefenbaker/Kennedy years."

I reminded Sharp that if something were to happen in Argentia, neither the United States defence strategy nor the state of Canada/ US relations would be uppermost in the minds of Newfoundlanders. "Before they know what's happening, they'll all be blown to kingdom come," I said.

Trying not to be overheard by the media people, who congregate after Question Period in the area just outside the Commons Chamber, Sharp continued whispering as he and I walked towards the outer door of the Parliament Building. Once outside and away from the media, Sharp continued to lambaste me for having asked the question.

Finally, with my patience reaching the breaking point, I said, "What in hell do you expect me to do—get on my knees and thank you and your government for turning my province into a nuclear weapons arsenal? If you dared to give the Americans permission to stockpile nuclear weapons in any other Canadian province, not only would there be hell to pay, but it would bring down your government. What makes you think you can get away with it in Newfoundland?"

Walking back to my office in West Block, I tried to convince myself that Sharp had overreacted to my question. Perhaps he was trying to discourage me from pursuing the matter any further in the Commons or in the news media. However, as I entered my office and was told by my secretary that the Speaker, Lucien Lamoureux, was very anxious to speak with me on the telephone, I began to have second thoughts. "Maybe Sharp wasn't bluffing after all," I thought to myself.

I immediately phoned the Speaker's office and was put through to Lamoureux right away. He informed me that he had received a phone call from the Commissioner of the Royal Canadian Mounted Police immediately after Question Period, requesting permission for a senior officer to visit my office on Parliament Hill to discuss the contents of my question to the Secretary of State for External Affairs.

Under the rules of the House of Commons, a police officer is not permitted to enter the precincts of the House of Commons to question a Member of Parliament without the Speaker's permission. Members enjoy certain rights, privileges and immunities, including immunity from arrest, as long as they remain within the precincts of the House. Also, if permission is granted to the RCMP to question a Member of Parliament, it must be done by an officer of no less rank than Superintendent.

I assured the Speaker that I had no objection to being questioned by an RCMP officer, providing a third person was present. The Speaker agreed and suggested that I prepare myself for a visit from a RCMP Superintendent later that afternoon.

As soon as I finished talking with the Speaker, I called Robert Stanfield and told him what was going on. I asked him to have someone present in my office during the meeting. I suggested that Eric Nielsen, a lawyer and a very good friend of mine, sit in. Stanfield agreed that a third party should be present and that Nielsen would be a good choice. He said he would have Nielsen come to my office right away to discuss the matter before the RCMP Superintendent arrived.

Eric Nielsen was one of the brightest and most politically astute members of the Conservative caucus. He was elected and re-elected to represent the Yukon riding in the House of Commons in twelve elections. A decorated World War Two fighter pilot, Nielsen was noted for being gutsy, no-nonsense, and not easy to intimidate.

An avowed nationalist and admirer of John Diefenbaker, Nielsen felt strongly about Canadian sovereignty and the extent to which Canada's foreign and domestic policies were being influenced by the Americans. He was also a staunch defender of the long-established right of Members of Parlia-

ment to speak freely in Parliament without fear of intimida-
tion or silencing by anyone, including the RCMP.

Nielsen was in the Chamber when I questioned Sharp. He
saw nothing wrong with my question. In fact, he considered it
my duty to ask the question once the matter came to my
attention. To deliberately withhold such information would
be placing myself in the position of being party to a cover-up,
he said.

I had the distinct feeling that the RCMP Superintendent
who came to my office later that afternoon was not too
enamoured of politicians or the special privileges they enjoyed. The nature of his questions and his condescending
manner convinced me that he would stop at nothing to obtain
the information he was after, namely, the identity of my
informant.

Having already been advised by Nielsen to let the officer
do most of the talking, I sat in my chair like a piece of granite
while he subtly tried to convince me that I faced dire consequences if I refused to cooperate. Sensing that Nielsen was
reaching the boiling point, I told the officer that he was
wasting both his and our time. "Under no circumstances will
I tell you where I got the information," I stated. "And that's
that."

I reminded him that as a Member of Parliament I enjoyed
certain rights and privileges, including the right to speak
freely on the floor of the House of Commons with complete
immunity. With that, he became belligerent and, in a threatening tone of voice, said it would be in my best interest to
cooperate.

Nielsen and I had already agreed that he would intervene
only if the RCMP Superintendent stepped out of line and
became too pushy. The moment that happened, I would
allow Nielsen to take over. Obviously, the RCMP Officer's
veiled threat hit a raw nerve. Nielsen, who had been sitting
back taking it all in, stood up, walked over to the Officer, took

him by the arm, and led him to the door. In a tone that left no doubt he meant business, Nielsen said, "You have asked your last question; this meeting is over." Before the officer had a chance to object, Nielsen added, "Either you leave this office immediately, or I will have you removed. Which will it be?"

The officer hesitated for a moment, gave Nielsen and me a dirty look, and left.

I shall probably never know the full extent of the fallout that resulted from my question to the Secretary of State for External Affairs. Two things happened subsequent to the incident which caused me considerable concern. I have reason to believe that the telephone in my Ottawa office was bugged for several days. Secondly, visits at the US Naval Base in Argentia were significantly less pleasant and relaxing. I had the distinct impression that I was constantly under surveillance. That was later confirmed by a senior US Naval Officer who was stationed at Argentia when the incident took place. He confided to me one evening over a drink at the Officer's Club that my movements on the base were being constantly monitored.

As a Member of Parliament, it would have been difficult for Base authorities to bar me completely from the Base. I had done nothing except condemn our federal government for having arbitrarily sanctioned an action taken by a foreign power that jeopardized the existence of every living organism in that part of our province, indeed perhaps in Newfoundland. Tens of thousands of Newfoundlanders were placed in the high-risk situation of having to live constantly with an arsenal of nuclear weapons capable of obliterating the entire Avalon Peninsula from the face of the planet. They were also in the untenable position of being a likely target in the event of a nuclear missile attack by the Soviet Union which, at that time, seemed a distinct possibility.

Twenty-eight

The Icelandic Cod War

I have a warm spot in my heart for Iceland and for the Icelandic people. It began back in 1970 when I first visited that country as a Member of the Canadian House of Commons. I visited Iceland again in 1982, as a member of the Canadian delegation to the founding meeting of the North Atlantic Salmon Conservation Organization. That organization was founded by salmon conservationists in Europe, the United States and Canada. Its mandate was to negotiate an international treaty for the conservation and management of North Atlantic salmon.

One of the driving forces behind the 1982 conference in Iceland and the move to negotiate a salmon management treaty was Dick Buck, a well known American conservationist and special advisor to President Ronald Reagan. Buck, who at that time was in his mid-seventies, was an extremely interesting person. We became very good friends. He was a great storyteller. In the evenings, a small group of us would sit around the huge stone fireplace in the lobby of the hotel in Reykjavik and listen attentively as Buck entertained us with his stories. Dick Buck was, it seems, a lifelong friend of Ronald Reagan and a regular visitor to the White House during Reagan's tenure as President.

My next visit to Iceland was in 1992 as Newfoundland's Minister of Fisheries. Following his visit to Newfoundland the previous year, Iceland's Minister of Fisheries invited me to attend an international trade exhibition there as guest of the Icelandic government.

Taken at a reception in Iceland, 1992. Left to right: President of
Iceland; Walter Carter; Icelandic Minister of Fisheries

I arrived in time for the official opening of the exhibition
by President Vigdis Finnbogadottir. I was deeply touched
when she introduced me as "a great friend of the people of
Iceland." She went on to describe how, in 1970, I and three
other Newfoundland Members of Parliament stood up in the
Canadian House of Commons and supported Iceland in its
struggle with the British to save Icelandic fisheries from
extinction. President Finnbogadottir who, in 1980, became
the world's first female president, then referred to our visit to
Iceland and subsequently to Great Britain where, she said,
"Mr. Carter and his three colleagues courageously stood their
ground and defended the action taken by the Icelandic
government against the British."

She was referring, of course, to an incident that took place
in the late 1960s, when Iceland found itself embroiled in a
cod war with Great Britain. It all started when British fishing
interests, supported by the British government, refused to
cooperate with the Government of Iceland's efforts to stave
off the impending depletion of their cod stocks.

Icelanders are much like Newfoundlanders and Labradorians. They are down-to-earth, fiercely independent, gutsy
people. And, like Newfoundlanders and Labradorians, they
have a long history of battling the elements and contending
with greedy, self-serving fishing interests who, like high-seas
pirates, plundered their fish stocks almost to the brink of
extinction.

In the late 1960s, the people of Iceland were desperate.
The rich cod and herring fishing grounds from which Icelanders derived 80% of their income were being pillaged by
British fishing interests at such a rate that the resource would
soon be depleted. Unlike the situation in Canada and in
other industrialized countries, where workers enjoy the security of generous social programs to tide them over in times of
crisis, without the fisheries the Icelandic government was
unable to provide a long-term social safety net for its people.
If the British continued to overfish in its waters, Iceland's only
hope for survival was to declare sovereignty over its continental shelf and assume exclusive rights to manage and control
its fisheries.

That is precisely what Iceland did. In 1969, it served
notice on the international community that it intended to
declare sovereignty over its continental shelf and assume
exclusive control over its fisheries. Only fish that were surplus
to the needs of Icelanders would be accessible to outside
interests. Because they have long regarded the waters off
Iceland as an important fishing ground for their own fleet,
the British were outraged. They not only refused to take the
Government of Iceland seriously, but they refused to take
seriously the right of any coastal state to unilaterally declare
sovereignty over its fisheries.

It did not take long, however, for the British fishing vessel
owners and their skippers, who continued to fish in Icelandic
waters, to find out just how serious the Icelanders were and

the extent to which they were prepared to go to defend their government's actions.

In makeshift gunboats, the people of that barren, wind-swept little island, with a population only slightly larger than that of St. John's, took on the British fishing fleet and literally booted them out. At one point, ships of the Royal Navy had to be sent in to protect the British trawlers from the Icelanders; those too were booted out.

With world opinion on their side, and with some sober second thoughts by the British, Iceland emerged the winner from the so-called "Cod War." Their right to unilaterally declare jurisdiction over their fisheries was recognized by the world community, and the task of rebuilding and properly managing their seriously ravaged fish stocks began in earnest.

At the time of the Icelandic Cod War, I was a Member of the Canadian House of Commons and Opposition spokesman for fisheries. Because of a close similarity to the situation in Newfoundland and Labrador, where foreign nationals were ravishing our fish stocks, I followed with considerable interest the events that were unfolding in Iceland and that country's approach to the problem of foreign overfishing. In fact, during that period, my Newfoundland colleagues and I were waging our own battle in the House of Commons. We were trying to get the Government of Canada to extend fisheries jurisdiction to the edge and the slopes of the Canadian continental shelf to protect our rapidly dwindling fish stocks from foreign overfishing. Whenever the House of Commons was in session, we were on our feet, needling the Prime Minister and demanding that he show the kind of courage demonstrated by his Icelandic counterpart.

In the spring of 1970—a few hours after one of our more raucous sessions in the Commons—my colleagues and I received a message from the Prime Minister of Iceland, thanking us for the manner in which we were supporting

Iceland's struggle to end overfishing. He invited us to visit his country as guests of the Icelandic government, in order to see firsthand what was happening.

Without consulting anyone (including Robert Stanfield, our Party leader) we accepted the Prime Minister's invitation. The following week, Newfoundland Tory Members of Parliament James McGrath, John Lundrigan, Jack Marshall and I arrived in Iceland where we were to spend the next several days up to our collective necks in the Cod War. The Government and people of Iceland treated us royally. Upon our arrival at the Reykjavik airport, we were met by the Prime Minister and a senior member of his staff, assigned to look after us during our stay.

The following day we spent several hours meeting with the Prime Minister and members of his Cabinet, comparing notes on the problems that plagued our respective fisheries—not the least of which was foreign overfishing. It soon became obvious that supporting the Icelandic position, even though it was against our mother country, was the right thing to do.

During the next four days we were taken on several whirlwind tours of various institutions and historic sites. We visited fish processing plants where we talked to the workers, most of whom were clean-cut, healthy-looking high school students who sang lustily as they went about their work of cutting and packing fish. We were surprised to learn that to avoid interfering with the quality of their education system, school authorities in Iceland arranged their school year so that students were able to work in fish processing plants in early spring when the days are long and jobs are plentiful.

Education levels are high in Iceland, where more books and newspapers are purchased per person than in any other country in the world. Our visit to Iceland's Fisheries Institute was a real eye opener. We were introduced to members of the staff who had at their disposal the world's most advanced

Taken onboard Icelandic Gunboat In 1969. Left to right: Walter Carter;
Jack Marshall; Icelandic Government official; John Lundrigan

research and technological capability. Many of them had
university degrees in almost every discipline in marine sci-
ence, and they spent a lifetime concentrating their studies
and research, sometimes on a single species of fish. One
person I met was introduced as "Dr. Capelin." He derived his
nickname by virtue of the fact that his entire academic career
was spent conducting research on capelin.

Another interesting aspect of our visit to Iceland was a
trip up the Icelandic coast aboard one of the gunboats being
used to oust both the British fishing vessels and the Royal
Navy. Not much larger than a typical Newfoundland
longliner, these boats featured a single cannon mounted on
the foredeck, augmented by the antiquated, scissor-like ap-
paratus used for cutting the warps off the fishing nets. These
little vessels and their courageous crews made life so unbearable for the skippers of the British trawlers, and so costly for
their owners, that they were forced to cease fishing and return
home.

On the last evening of our visit, the Speaker of the

Althing, or Parliament, accompanied us on a tour of the site of the first Althing, appropriately named the "cradle of democracy," where, in 930 A.D., the first democratically elected parliament in the world deliberated. Later that evening, the Prime Minister of Iceland hosted a state dinner in our honour.

The Icelandic news media gave our visit complete coverage; every move we made was reported in the press. Naturally, the presence of four Canadian Members of Parliament in a foreign country, supporting its fishermen in a dispute with their mother country, also aroused considerable attention in both Canadian and British newspapers. The day before we were to return to Canada, we were surprised to receive a message from Lady Tweedsmuir, Britain's Minister of Fisheries, inviting us to London to hear Britain's side of the Cod War story. Marshall, Lundrigan and I accepted Lady Tweedsmuir's invitation and left the next morning for London. For personal reasons, Jim McGrath had to decline Lady Tweedsmuir's invitation and return to Ottawa.

Not to be outdone by the government of Iceland, Great Britain rolled out the red carpet. As the British Airways jumbo jet that flew us to London halted in front of the Heathrow terminal building, we were met by British government officials wearing spats, black jackets, striped trousers and black bowler hats. Without having to retrieve our luggage or clear it through customs, we were immediately whisked away in a black limousine to Claridge's Hotel (the most prestigious hotel in England) where we spent the next four days living in the lap of luxury as guests of the British.

That evening we were invited to a dinner party hosted by a senior official of the British Department of Fisheries, in a private dining room on the top floor of the hotel. The following morning we were chauffeured to the Parliament buildings, where Lady Tweedsmuir introduced us to several of her colleagues and senior officials of the British Govern-

ment. In the afternoon she arranged for us to sit in the
Speaker's Gallery of the House of Commons, where we were
introduced by the Speaker and given a warm welcome by the
British MPs who, in their typically polite way, shouted "Hear!
Hear!" as the Speaker welcomed us to the Chamber.

The Speaker then called Oral Questions. The lead-off
question by the Leader of the Opposition had to do with the
dispute between Britain and Iceland over fisheries jurisdiction and the government's response to the pro-Icelandic
position taken by the visiting delegation of Canadian Parliamentarians.

Prime Minister Heath was visibly annoyed with the question. I had the uncomfortable feeling that he was equally
annoyed by our presence, not only in the Speaker's Gallery
but in Britain itself. Looking directly at us, he said, "Since my
Minister of Fisheries will be making a statement later this
afternoon on the subject matter of the Honourable Gentleman's question, I do not intend to debate with Honourable
Members opposite the merits of my Government's position
on the Icelandic situation or their interpretation of the
position taken by the visiting Canadian Parliamentarians."

Following Question Period, Lady Tweedsmuir stood and
announced that the government's white paper on the fisheries dispute between Iceland and Great Britain would be
tabled in the House Thursday afternoon and made available
to the news media at a press conference planned for later that
day. Returning to our hotel later that afternoon, we were
handed a message from Lady Tweedsmuir, inviting us to
attend her press conference.

On the second evening of our visit to London, Lord and
Lady Tweedsmuir hosted an official banquet at Manchester
House in our honour. Several members of the British Cabinet
were in attendance, including the former Prime Minister, Sir
Alec Douglas-Hume who, at that time, was a senior Minister
in the Heath Cabinet. I was seated next to Sir Alec at the head

table. As we were eating, he turned to me and said in his flawless Oxford accent, "I say, old chap, if you were in my position, what would be your advice to the Prime Minister as to how we can extricate ourselves from this bloody mess we are in with the Icelanders?"

Flattered to have been asked for advice by a former Prime Minister of Great Britain, I welcomed the opportunity to articulate my views on the Cod War, and defend the right of Iceland and all other coastal states to manage and control their fisheries. I suggested to Sir Alec that if I were in his position, my advice to Prime Minister Heath would be to acknowledge Iceland's right to declare sovereignty over its continental shelf, and order all British fishing vessels out of Icelandic waters. I would also advise him to order the Royal Navy to stop harassing Icelandic fishermen and return to home base immediately. "It disappoints me," I said, "to see Great Britain, the bastion of democracy and common justice, using the awesome might of the Royal Navy to crush a mere handful of Icelandic fishermen who ask nothing more than the right to survive." Finally, I reminded Sir Alec, "Unlike the British Commonwealth, where almost every natural resource known to mankind is in abundance, Iceland's survival depends solely on its fisheries. Without it they will perish," I said.

Sir Alec listened attentively to what I was saying. Looking directly at me, he paused for a moment and said, "By Jove, old chap, you hit the nail squarely on the head—that is precisely the advice I intended to give Heath when we meet later this evening."

Obviously, my conversation with Sir Alec Douglas Hume did not go down well with our host. The next morning we received a message from Lady Tweedsmuir, informing us that the invitation to attend her press conference was withdrawn. She was concerned, she said, that she would be unable to justify inviting three Canadian Members of Parliament to her press conference, having earlier refused to extend the same courtesy to members of her own caucus.

We were convinced that she had other reasons for not wanting us there. Maybe she was unprepared to risk having three loose cannons, whose views on her government's fisheries dispute with Iceland were not entirely pro-British, mingling with members of the British press.

In a way, we were relieved. Since our sympathies were still with the fishermen of Iceland, it would have been very difficult for us to sit through Lady Tweedsmuir's press conference and not speak out against Great Britain's high-handed approach towards the Icelandic fisheries problem. We decided then and there to call our own press conference and express our views on the situation.

In a room less than 50 feet from Lady Tweedsmuir's scheduled press conference, we met members of the British press and told them in no uncertain terms where we stood on the Cod War issue. We compared the plight of the Icelandic people to that of the people of Newfoundland. "In both cases," we said, "our most important resource, the fisheries, is being destroyed by greedy, self-serving foreign nationals, who continue to ravage the stocks without regard for the rights of the indigenous coastal states whose people are facing economic disaster."

We reminded the British press that, while "the Icelanders have the British to deal with, we have to contend with vessels from numerous other countries, including Britain, who continue to plunder our fish stocks like high-seas pirates."

The media people liked what we were saying, and they obviously liked the way we said it. The next morning the London papers gave us considerably more coverage than they gave Lady Tweedsmuir's White Paper briefing.

We felt good about the outcome of our press conference. The media people were obviously impressed with our blunt and somewhat colourful replies to their questions. However, we soon found out that Lady Tweedsmuir and her officials were not impressed.

When we returned to our hotel, we were informed that the special privileges extended to us by the British government when we arrived in London, including the use of a chauffeur-driven car and a shopping guide, were discontinued. We also found out that an official from Lady Tweedsmuir's department had already advised the hotel management that, as of checkout time the following day, they would not be responsible for any charges incurred by us, including the cost of our rooms. More simply put, we were getting the royal boot.

By virtue of Jack Marshall's wartime rank in the Army—that of a full-fledged Colonel—the officials assigned by Lady Tweedsmuir to look after us had assumed that he was our leader. Their initial contact with us when we were in Iceland and the arrangements for our visit to London were made through "The Colonel." When the time came to check us out of our suites and settle our accounts with the hotel, they contacted The Colonel.

Because of the rapid deterioration of our relationship with Lady Tweedsmuir and her officials, and the hassle over who should accept responsibility for certain charges, Lundrigan and I were more than willing to defer to The Colonel. In fact, we were very pleased that Marshall had retired from the Army with the rank of Colonel, and not Corporal.

As we headed toward the elevator, struggling with our overstuffed suitcases, Lundrigan was philosophical. In his Island Cove accent, he said, "A few hours ago, old cock, we were peacocks, wined and dined at Manchester House; hobnobbing with cabinet ministers, including a former Prime Minister; introduced in the House of Commons by the Speaker; and chauffeured around London in a Rolls Royce. But look at us now—a couple of old feather dusters."

As we got off the crowded elevator and stepped into the

hotel lobby, we could not control our laughter. Standing in the crowded lobby of Britain's most elegant and prestigious hotel, surrounded by curious onlookers, was our colleague "Colonel" Marshall, visibly angry and embroiled in a heated argument with an official of Lady Tweedsmuir's office, who stubbornly refused to accept responsibility for a $10 long-distance call that Marshall made to his Ottawa office earlier that day.

Unlike the red carpet treatment accorded us when we arrived at Heathrow Airport a few days earlier, our departure was much less pretentious. With barely enough British currency between us to pay the taxi fare to the airport, we came close to having to thumb a ride. As we boarded the aircraft for our return flight to Ottawa, the flight attendant handed me a copy of a London newspaper. The headline read, "Prime Minister Orders Navy Home." I cannot speak for my colleagues, Marshall and Lundrigan, but whenever I am tempted to take credit for that headline, I remind myself of the words of St. Augustine, "It is pride that changes angels into devils; it is humility that makes a man an angel."

Twenty-nine

Tales from the Dorval Lounge

When I was first elected to the House of Commons in 1968, Members of Parliament received an annual salary of $12,000, plus a tax-free expense allowance of $6,000. Members were assigned an office on Parliament Hill, a secretary, and unrestricted access to a pool of professional researchers and speech writers. We also had access to what is undoubtedly the best library in Canada, and a reading room where Members and their aides had access to current copies of all major Canadian and US newspapers and magazines.

There were other benefits too: free travel anywhere in Canada on Canadian National and Canadian Pacific Railway systems for Members and their families; a weekly airline ticket to and from our constituencies; and a pass that provided us with access to all first-class lounges operated by Canadian owned airlines anywhere in the world.

Those of us who represented constituencies in more remote regions were undoubtedly the most travelled workers in this country. For at least nine months of the year, we spent from Monday to Friday in Ottawa attending to our duties in the House of Commons and weekends travelling in our constituencies where most of us continued to maintain a permanent residence.

I have since regretted that I did not keep a record of the number of times I commuted to and from Ottawa and St. John's during my three terms in the House of Commons. It must have been at least four hundred times. Almost every Friday afternoon I would join the exodus of Members of

Parliament who scurried from their offices on Parliament Hill to the Ottawa airport to catch a flight to their constituencies.

Since there were very few direct flights originating in Ottawa to cities in Atlantic Canada, those of us heading in that direction would have to go to Montreal to catch a connecting flight to our home provinces. The return trip usually included a Montreal stopover too.

The duration of our stopover in Montreal varied—it was seldom less than an hour and, depending on the weather and volume of traffic, it was frequently prolonged to several hours. Having access to the visitors' lounges at Dorval Airport was a blessing. It was a place to go, away from the pandemonium that usually existed at Dorval on Fridays, and relax in comfort.

Most Members of Parliament who were forced to stop over at Dorval, especially on Friday evening, gravitated toward the Air Canada lounge where they would have a drink, talk shop and enjoy a unique esprit de corps.

Human nature being what it is, there were times when Members of Parliament abused the privilege and overstayed their welcome in the various airline lounges, more particularly the one in Montreal. A certain well known Member of Parliament who represented a constituency in the Atlantic region would often arrive in Dorval Airport on his way back to Ottawa on Monday morning and remain there most of the day enjoying Air Canada's hospitality, including free booze. He would arrive in Ottawa several hours later in a drunken stupor, and go directly to the House of Commons where he would stand in his place and proceed to make a rousing speech.

Since it was never intended to be a hangout, or an unlimited source of free booze for first-class airline patrons, the majority of us who frequented the various airline lounges appreciated the privilege and respected the spirit in which it was accorded to us. That is not to suggest, however, that we objected too strenuously about the delays we frequently experienced on our way to our constituencies on Friday evenings.

The Dorval lounge was a most exciting and interesting place to visit. Frequently, world leaders, movie stars and other international celebrities would drop in between flights to enjoy a drink and a few minutes of relaxation away from the crowds.

I had an encounter there one evening with comedian Jerry Lewis. I was sitting in the lounge with a colleague waiting to connect with a flight to Ottawa when suddenly there was a commotion near the reception area. Jerry Lewis and his entourage had just arrived in Montreal on an overseas flight from Europe and were being whisked into the lounge by an Air Canada attendant. Lewis was carrying an oversize briefcase, almost like an old fashioned cardboard suitcase, that he securely held under his arm as he was escorted to a table a few yards from where we were seated.

The extent to which he was guarding the suitcase aroused my curiosity, and no doubt the curiosity of the other people present. He clowned around in an obvious attempt to attract attention to himself and the thing he was carrying. Even after he was seated, he continued to keep it by his side. What is in that suitcase that would cause him to be be treating it with such care? I wondered, as he continued to hug it close to his side. I did not have to wait long to find out. With every eye in the lounge focused on him, he planked the suitcase on the table, unlocked it for all to see and slowly removed its contents and piled it on the table.

The suitcase was chock full of money. Hundreds, maybe thousands of bills neatly stacked and kept together with rubber bands. I couldn't help wonder why a man of Lewis's obvious means was (seemingly) forced to carry his money about in such an awkward fashion. From the time Lewis and his party arrived until they left an hour later, the place was in turmoil. I was never a great fan of Jerry Lewis; I always considered him to be an egotistical show-off. His behaviour that evening confirmed my impression of him. When he was satisfied that the onlookers were suitably impressed, he instructed a member of his entourage to put the money back in the suitcase, and in a loud voice cautioned him to make sure that it was all there. Lewis then got up and started to walk around the lounge and show off for the benefit of the Air Canada hostesses and the other guests who were standing around gawking at him and waiting to get his autograph.

My colleague and I deliberately remained seated at our table and continued our discussion without paying any attention to what was going on around us. Maybe our apparent lack of interest intrigued Lewis because he came over to where we were seated. He leaned over our table and stared at us for a minute or two in complete silence, as if waiting for us to recognize him or ask for his autograph. We pretended we did not know who he was. We then spoke to him briefly and casually commented about the weather. He remained leaning over our table staring at us in complete silence.

Finally I said, "I swear I have seen you somewhere before. Don't tell me your name...let me guess." After an appropriate pause, I said, "Have you ever been on television?"

I am not sure if it was anger or simply the symptoms of a badly deflated ego, but he was obviously annoyed. He continued to stare at me without saying a word as I went through the pretence of not knowing who he was.

Suddenly, I took his hand and said, "I have it—I know where I saw you; it was on television with Dean Martin. You're Dean Martin's sidekick, right?"

He was not amused. Unlike his television persona—a supremely confident person with a great sense of humor—he stood there for a few seconds licking out his tongue and making faces at us. He then turned around and walked back to his table.

A few days later I read a story in a tabloid about the breakup of the long-standing comedy team of Dean Martin and Jerry Lewis. In typical tabloid fashion, it gave all the gory details of the breakup and the bad blood that existed between the two comedians as a result. I realized then that Jerry Lewis' response to my smart-ass behaviour a few days earlier was understandable.

There were others, too, who obviously enjoyed Air Canada's hospitality. One such frequent Air Canada flyer and visitor to the lounge was a prominent Newfoundland businessman whose interests required him to commute between Montreal and St. John's on a regular basis. For a while, it seemed that every time I walked into the lounge in Montreal airport he was there having a drink, usually surrounded by several of his business associates. A loud, boisterous individual, he never let the opportunity pass to voice his opinion of politicians, always in a not too complimentary way.

Whenever I entered the Lounge and saw him there I cringed. Invariably, the moment he spotted me he would unleash a tirade of nasty, demeaning comments about politicians, most of which were directed at me personally, since I represented the constituency in which he voted. That, coupled with the fact that he was a substantial corporate taxpayer, gave him license, he thought, to berate me like any other employee. He seemed to derive a perverse sense of satisfaction from doing this.

Speaking in a tone of voice that caused other people in the Lounge to perk up and take notice, he usually started by asking me what I had done during the past week to earn my salary. He would then launch into a tirade about what it was costing him and the rest of the country to pay politicians their "exorbitant salaries and all kinds of perks for sitting on their asses in the House of Commons and doing nothing."

While I would try my best not to let him get under my skin, I have to admit there were times when it was difficult to ignore his abusive and insulting comments. However, since he was noted for being a loudmouth, rather than cause a scene I would laugh with the others and treat him and his verbal abuse for what it was worth. Obviously, the people around him also knew him for what he was because they also seemed embarrassed by his intemperate behavior and uncalled-for insults. Meanwhile, others in the lounge, some of whom I knew, would giggle and appear to enjoy his antics at my expense.

On my way to Newfoundland one Friday evening, my stopover in Montreal was longer than expected. I instinctively headed for the lounge where I would be kept informed as to my departure and maybe meet a few of my colleagues and have a drink. Other flights to the Atlantic Provinces were also delayed that evening; when I entered the lounge several of my colleagues were already there.

Also seated having a drink with several of his business associates was the St. John's businessman whom I referred to above. The moment he eyed me he could hardly wait to take his usual verbal swipe. "Well, well," he shouted, "look who just walked in, the Honourable Member for St. John's West. Tell me," he said, "what have you and your parasitical buddies done this week to earn the fat salaries you are collecting from the taxpayers of Canada. Since I am one of the voters in St. John's West who is contributing to your upkeep, I have a right to know what you have been doing."

I was not sure whether it was the quality or the quantity of the Scotch he was drinking, but that evening he was louder than usual and decidedly more insulting. He also had a larger than usual audience.

After he berated me for several minutes, I quietly asked him if he was finished because if he was, there was something I wanted to say. When I was sure that I had their attention, I told the other people in the lounge, who by this time were thoroughly enjoying the spectacle, that what they were witnessing was a common occurrence. I told them that the gentleman in question was a wealthy, fellow Newfoundlander whose impressions of politics and politicians was somewhat less than flattering. "In fact they are downright insulting," I said.

I went on to say that this was not the first time he accosted me in front of an audience and complained that his tax dollars were being squandered. I then looked directly at him and in a very reasoned tone said, "In the district of St. John's West, which I represent in the House of Commons there are fifty thousand voters including yourself."

I told him what I was being paid, which at that time was $25,000 a year. "If you divide one into the other," I said, "you will see that it cost you fifty cents a year to have me represent you in the House of Commons." I then put my hand in my pocket and took out two quarters. "I have decided," I said, "that for a lousy fifty cents I am not going to spend the next twelve months putting up with your crap—it's simply not worth it."

With that I reached over and put two quarters in front of him on his table. I said, "I am giving you back your money. For the remainder of this term I will cost you nothing, and I will owe you nothing. So, as of this moment don't ever speak to me in that tone of voice again. Stick your fifty cents up your ass and keep your big mouth shut."

In my political career I have on occasion welcomed the uplifting experience that one gets from a hearty round of applause. However, none was as uplifting or as welcomed as the round of applause I received that evening in the Air Canada lounge in Montreal.

Since the gentleman referred to here has long since gone to his just reward, it would serve no useful purpose for me to reveal his earthly identity. Suffice to say, I pray that he is now in heaven with the saints, no longer paying taxes or having to contribute to the "fat salaries of overpaid, underworked politicians." However, I am sometimes tempted to pray that as a fitting reward for his self-confessed hatred of politicians, if there are elevators in heaven, he spend eternity stuck between floors with John Diefenbaker and Joey Smallwood.

Thirty

Saving President Nixon's Life?

The afternoon sitting of the Canadian House of Commons on April 14, 1972 was a historic occasion. I sat almost directly across the aisle of the Commons Chamber from Prime Minister Pierre Elliott Trudeau as he welcomed the President of the United States, Richard M. Nixon, to the House of Commons. Sitting two seats ahead of me was former Prime Minister John G. Diefenbaker who, a decade earlier, had welcomed another American President, John F. Kennedy, to Canada.

In welcoming President Nixon, Prime Minister Trudeau was at his best. "You see before you, Mr. President," he said, "Canadians from every corner of this far-flung land we call Canada. They reflect, not just the geography of the country, but also the great mixture of peoples that adds such variety and richness to our national life. The different origins of many of these men and women, and the languages they speak, illustrate the diversity of Canada."

Later that afternoon, Members of Parliament and Senators were given the opportunity to meet President and Mrs. Nixon in the House of Commons foyer. That evening the Government of Canada hosted a gala concert at the National Arts Centre, featuring artists from each of the ten provinces and the territories. They performed for the presidential party and local dignitaries, including Members of Parliament, the Senate and the Judiciary. President and Mrs. Nixon were seated with the Trudeaus at front row centre, flanked by senior members of the presidential party and members of the federal Cabinet. Members of Parliament and Senators were seated in alphabetical order directly behind the visiting dignitaries, which placed me in the third row, directly behind President Nixon.

Taking everything in from a back-row seat in the National Arts Centre was Arthur H. Bremer, a twenty-one-year-old native of Milwaukee, Wisconsin, who had arrived in Canada from the States a few hours earlier for the express purpose of assassinating President Nixon. A month later in a crowded courtroom in Maryland, Bremer was convicted and subsequently sentenced to 53 years in prison for gunning down Alabama Governor George C. Wallace.

FBI agents and Maryland police investigating the Wallace shooting found evidence that Bremer had stalked President Nixon during his official visit to Canada on April 13-15, waiting for an opportunity to assassinate him. They identified Bremer in a picture in an Ottawa newspaper, standing in a crowd that had gathered to welcome President Nixon as he arrived on Parliament Hill to address a joint sitting of the Senate and the House of Commons.

Entries in Bremer's diary, written as he zigzagged across the States and Canada in pursuit of his victim, told how he had entered Canada three days before Nixon's visit, with weapons hidden in his car. He wrote: "I instantly lost all respect for the 'Big Bad Canadian Customs'.... I could have had enough guns in my car to start a revolution and twelve pygmies to carry them all on their heads."

The diary, read by a State attorney to jurors in Bremer's trial on charges arising from the shooting of Wallace at a political rally in Maryland on May 15, 1972, told of six narrowly missed chances to shoot President Nixon while he was in Ottawa.

Bremer wrote: "From the very beginning I planned to get him at the airport addressing a happy Canadian crowd." But when he was refused admittance to the airport, a policeman directed Bremer to another point on the Nixon motorcade route. When he arrived there, a policeman was standing near the President. "I fantasized killing Nixon while shooting over that cop's shoulder," Bremer wrote, "but the chance was missed because I was uncertain whether the bullets from my .38-calibre revolver would penetrate the glass of Nixon's limousine. I didn't want to get killed or imprisoned in an unsuccessful attempt."

He also wrote that he had waited, with a gun in his pocket, for President Nixon's motorcade to arrive on Parliament Hill. "Everything happened so fast," he wrote, "before I knew it, like a snap of the finger, he was gone and again I missed my chance to kill him."

That evening, as President and Mrs. Nixon arrived at the National Arts Centre to attend the concert planned in their honour, Bremer was already there, patiently awaiting the opportunity to carry out his mission. "This time," he thought, "nothing will get in the way. Nixon will soon be history, and I will have earned my place in American history as his assassin."

Following his arrest for the Wallace shooting, Bremer told police what actually had gotten in the way, foiling his attempt to assassinate the President. Apparently he intended to shoot the President from his seat in the back of the National Arts Centre. He told the police, "Every time I tried to get a bead on Nixon, the fellow sitting behind him would get in the way. The guy must have had the fidgets. He kept shifting positions, and his big head blocked my view."

Admittedly, my claim to having saved President Nixon's life is based on circumstantial evidence and is not likely to win me the US Congressional Medal of Honour or lead to a statue being erected in my honour on Parliament Hill. However, there are certain indisputable facts that must be recognized.

I was seated directly behind President Nixon on the night in question. I am noted for being fidgety when I sit in the

same position for long periods. My mother used to say, "You're like a cat on hot rocks." As for Bremer's reference to the man with the "big head" who kept getting in the way as he tried to take aim at Nixon, my hat size is seven-and-three-quarters and, at the time, I had a full head of curly hair.

Circumstantial evidence, you say. Maybe so. But who knows—perhaps if it were not for my big head and the fidgets, there would have been no Watergate scandal; the United States would still be up to its neck in the Vietnam War; and Gerald R. Ford's pension would now be based on his years of service in the Senate and not on his stint as President of the United States of America.

Thirty-one

A National Joke

On April 1, 1974, my colleagues and I accompanied Robert Stanfield, leader of Canada's Progressive Conservative Party, to St. John's, where we were invited to take part in the celebrations marking the 25th anniversary of Confederation. Several events were planned for the occasion, including a dinner hosted by the Government of Newfoundland and Labrador, and a special sitting of the House of Assembly in the Colonial Building, where the Newfoundland Legislature sat prior to the completion of the new chamber in Confederation Building in 1959.

At the time, I found it extremely difficult to get worked up over such celebrations. I had no quarrel with the notion that we should do something special to mark the occasion. However, after sitting in the House of Commons for the previous six years, and witnessing firsthand the arrogant and indifferent attitude of the central provinces and the national government towards Newfoundland and Labrador, I was not convinced that there was much to celebrate. It was difficult to feel good about being part of a country that was content to twiddle its thumbs while foreign nationals blatantly violated our sovereignty as a coastal state and brazenly plundered, almost to the brink of extinction, the resource on which our survival as a people depended.

Those of us who were elected under the Progressive Conservative banner in 1968 to represent Newfoundland and Labrador went to Ottawa that fall with a common cause. We were determined, come hell or high water, to force the

238

Trudeau government to take the necessary action to protect our rapidly dwindling northern cod stock. Extended jurisdiction to the edge and slopes of the Canadian continental shelf was the only real solution to the problem of foreign overfishing. We were prepared to use every device at our disposal, including exploiting the national press, to bring that about.

Our repeated requests for a special debate in the House of Commons on the issue of foreign overfishing, and our questions in the Commons to Prime Minister Trudeau and his Minister of Fisheries, Jack Davis, were futile. The Trudeau government downplayed the issue and stubbornly refused to be drawn into a debate. It soon became obvious that they were more concerned about protecting the manufacturing industry in Ontario's "Golden Triangle" and the economy of central Canada than the future well-being of a half million Newfoundlanders and Labradorians.

When it was decided that our National Party Leader would be visiting Newfoundland to take part in the celebrations, accompanied by a large contingent of the national media, we decided to make the most of their presence in Newfoundland to focus national attention on foreign overfishing. The idea originated with John Lundrigan, the Member of Parliament for Gander-Twillingate. He shared my view that nothing less than extended fisheries jurisdiction would remedy the problem.

Lundrigan was a superb politician. A former university professor, he was young and extremely bright. He also had the instincts of an Irish setter when it came to sniffing out political issues. Knowing how to attract media attention, he was on a friendly, first-name basis with most of the parliamentary press gallery members. In fact, as we were to find out, perhaps in this case he was a little too friendly with the Ottawa press.

The plan was to fly Stanfield and members of the national press over the Hamilton Banks to see firsthand what was happening to our northern cod stocks. Our contacts at the federal Department of Fisheries were telling us that the Hamilton Banks—the spawning ground for the cod stocks on which the entire northeast coast of Newfoundland and communities on the Labrador coast depend—were teeming with huge, ice-reinforced Russian and East German factory ships operating on a load-and-go basis. We discussed the idea with our colleagues, Jim McGrath, Member of Parliament for St. John's East, and Jack Marshall, Member of Parliament for Humber-St. George's-St. Barbe. Both liked the idea and volunteered to join us.

Lundrigan and I were delegated to make the arrangements. It was agreed that Lundrigan would discuss the matter with his friend, Bill Bennett, who owned a small airline company that operated out of Gander. Bennett's company owned several World War Two vintage aircraft, including an old DC-6 bomber which would be ideal for the flight because of its seating capacity. Perhaps, we thought, he will be willing to contribute to the cause by making it available to us at no cost. We cautioned Lundrigan to ensure that Bennett was fully aware of the situation. It would have to be *gratis*, because we had no way of accessing the money normally required to carry out such an undertaking. Lundrigan's telephone call to Bennett got results. Not only would he provide us with the old bomber, he would also be its pilot.

The following day, Lundrigan and I met with Stanfield in his Ottawa office and outlined our plan. To say that he did not jump for joy would be an understatement. At first, he merely sat and looked at us, as if he were waiting to be told it was all a big joke. What we were asking of him was completely foreign to his nature. Stanfield was extremely cautious and ultra-conservative when it came to doing anything that smacked of showmanship or raw politics. He abhorred theatrics and, much to the dismay of certain members of his caucus, refused to take part in anything that might be construed as such, especially by the national press.

At that time, Newfoundland members of the Conservative caucus were not part of Stanfield's inner circle. In fact, I sometimes had the feeling that he viewed us more as a nuisance than an asset. It began during the first session of Parliament following the 1968 general election. Our lack of decorum and irreverence soon won for the six of us the attention of mainland journalists and commentators, who referred to us as "the noisy six."

Writing in the *Toronto Globe and Mail* on February 6, 1969, in an article captioned, "Newfie 6; Upsetters of decorum," John Dafoe had this to say about our performance in the House of Commons: "Newfoundland's six 'wild and woolly' Conservative Members of Parliament appear to be making a hit with mainland journalists and commentators. They have approached Parliament with a lusty irreverence and a zest for battle that makes them the natural successors to the fighting Westerners of the past who have had a sudden attack of decorum and have lost their punch.... The role of 'upsetters of decorum' has been taken over by the Newfoundlanders."

While that kind of publicity in mainland and local newspapers was good for our ego and made great reading back in our constituencies, I am not sure it was appreciated by Stanfield and the staid, ultra-conservative, grey eminences of the Conservative caucus, whom Stanfield conferred with daily. Our so-called zest for debating the issues, the manner in which we collectively attacked the government and, when necessary, raised hell in the Commons, represented everything they abhorred.

After several meetings and considerable arm-twisting, Stanfield finally agreed to our plan. He reluctantly offered to accompany us on a flight over the Hamilton Banks. With only a couple of days remaining before Stanfield and his entourage were due to leave for St. John's, we turned our attention to members of the parliamentary press gallery. With Stanfield on side, we had no difficulty convincing them that it would be in their interest to cover our flight over the Hamilton Banks.

At the crack of dawn on March 31, a bevy of reporters and cameramen draped with cameras and the usual photographic paraphernalia, Stanfield, McGrath, Marshall, Lundrigan and myself boarded a plane in Gander and embarked on what turned out to be a six-hour comedy of errors, a colossal national joke. The age of the aircraft, its run-down condition, and the turbulence we encountered during takeoff were nerve-wrecking. To make matters worse, as the plane was taking off, Bob Stanfield's seat collapsed, throwing him with his legs in the air into the lap of newsman Charles Lynch, who was sitting directly behind him.

Sensing the passengers' discomfort and nervousness, and trying hard to suppress his own fear of flying, Lundrigan informed them that as soon as the aircraft levelled off, there would be a "screeching-in" ceremony. I should explain that screeching-in is an initiation ritual performed on visitors to Newfoundland and Labrador. They are required to swallow, not sip, about two ounces of Newfoundland Screech straight. The tradition started during World War Two.

Long before any liquor board was created to take alcohol under its benevolent wing, the Jamaican rum that would eventually be known as Screech was a mainstay of the Newfoundland diet. Salt fish was shipped to the West Indies in exchange for rum; the fish became the national dish of Jamaicans and the rum became the traditional drink of Newfoundlanders. It might have continued indefinitely as a nameless rum were it not for the influx of American servicemen to the Island during World War Two and an incident that occurred shortly after they arrived.

As the story goes, the commanding officer of the first detachment was taking advantage of Newfoundland hospital-

ity for the first time and was offered a drop of rum as an after-dinner drink. Seeing his Newfoundland host toss back the liquid straight without a quiver, the unsuspecting American felt obliged to do likewise and downed the drink in one gulp.

The look of shock and the colour of the American's face were overshadowed by the bloodcurdling howl made by the poor fellow as soon as he managed to regain his breath. One of the people who rushed to his assistance was a garrulous old American sergeant who pounded on the door and demanded to know, "What the cripes caused the Colonel to make that ungodly screech?" The person who answered the door, replied simply, "Tis the rum me son." Thus was born a legend. As word of the incident was passed around, the Americans determined to try this mysterious beverage that caused its victims to "screech." Finding its effects as devastating as the name implied, they adopted it as their favourite drink.

Bob Stanfield was Lundrigan's first screeching-in victim. Still not recovered from the jolt he experienced earlier when his seat collapsed, Stanfield looked anything but amused by Lundrigan's antics. Standing over Stanfield, like an impatient mother trying to get her child to take a tablespoon full of cod liver oil, Lundrigan handed him a water glass half-full of Screech and said, "Come on, Skipper Bob, down the hatch. This'll put hair on your chest."

People who know Bob Stanfield will agree that his lack of charisma is more than compensated by his dry sense of humour. After he recovered from the shock of the drink and was able to catch his breath, he rubbed his chin and drawled, "All right, Lundrigan, I'm ready for another one—but this time put some rum in it."

We spent six hours skimming the surface of the ice-infested North Atlantic, looking for Russian trawlers and evidence of foreign fishing activity, but the only vessel we saw was one engaged in repairing a transatlantic cable. Fortunately, the screeching-in ceremony, which Lundrigan deliberately prolonged, was having its effect on all of us, including Stanfield, who was very relaxed as he sang with the others a medley of Newfoundland folk songs. The atmosphere in the craft was like that of happy hour in a George Street bar. The only thing missing was a piano.

Finally, we had to call it a day and head back to St. John's, where we were to accompany Stanfield to a government-sponsored dinner at Hotel Newfoundland. As we were flying south over the North Atlantic, heading back to the St. John's airport, Stanfield left his seat in the rear of the plane and, trying to hide the effects of his screeching-in, slowly made his way up the aisle to the front.

Turning to face the others, he mimicked the Speaker of

the House of Commons, pretending to be straightening his robes. "Order! Order!" he shouted as loudly as he could to be heard over the noise of the engines. "Pursuant to Standing Order 26, I ask leave to present the following motion on a matter of urgent and pressing necessity: I move, seconded by the Honourable Member for St. John's East, that Carter and Lundrigan be requested to do the honourable thing and jump out. I further move that if they refuse to jump out voluntarily, we consider throwing them out. All those in favour, say aye." There was resounding approval of Stanfield's motion.

Sitting in the plane the next morning on our flight back to Ottawa, both Lundrigan and I agreed that we would have some explaining to do at our next weekly caucus and in the House of Commons. Not only did we make fools of ourselves, but we caused our Leader to make a fool of himself. And then, of course, we had to find a way to make amends with the members of the press gallery, whom we had encouraged to tag along at considerable expense and inconvenience.

There were other problems, as well. The outcome of our flight and the absence of foreign fishing effort in the area would damage our credibility in the eyes of our parliamentary colleagues and the national press. It would also weaken our case for government intervention to end foreign overfishing on the Hamilton Banks. As it was, our repeated efforts in the House of Commons to focus national attention on the problem of foreign overfishing (particularly on the prolific spawning grounds of the Hamilton Banks) were being constantly stonewalled by the Trudeau government. The Prime Minister and Minister of Fisheries were adamant: "Fish quotas allocated to foreign nationals and the rules under which they were being allocated are being strictly enforced."

Once the word got out that our flight over the Hamilton Banks did not produce the results we had hoped for, it would be easier for them to dismiss our claims and make it appear that the problem simply did not exist.

Fortunately, members of the national press who accompanied us on our ill-conceived flight were an exceptionally understanding group. They suspected from the start that the Russians had been tipped off and took steps to ensure that their fishing vessels were out of the area well in advance of our visit. It had been common knowledge in the National Press Club that we were planning the flight over the Hamilton Banks. Members of the Ottawa press corps were all too familiar with the leaks that frequently emanated from the National Press Club and ended up in the Russian Embassy.

As we discovered a few days later, they were right. The Russians knew what we were up to, and they acted accordingly. Over a drink at the National Press Club several days before we announced our planned flight, Lundrigan innocently mentioned it to a few of his media friends. It is a safe bet that the Russian Embassy learned of the plan and immediately alerted their Kremlin bosses.

Those of us who were travelling with Stanfield were booked to return to Ottawa the next day on the 6:30 a.m. flight. I intentionally checked out of the hotel early; I wanted to take a stroll to breathe the morning air and clear my head. I also needed time to think about the events of the previous day and perhaps find a way to make amends with Stanfield and the national media.

Stepping out on the sidewalk in front of the hotel, I saw Stanfield crouched down and stroking an old tomcat that was comfortably curled up on the sidewalk. I watched Stanfield from the shadows, as he and the cat appeared to be carrying on a conversation. Perhaps it was the aftereffects of too many drinks the night before, but I could have sworn they were talking to each other. The cat sounded almost human. In fact, its purring sounded more human and decidedly more pleasant to the ear than the sounds that sometimes came from members of the House of Commons.

Usually, Bob Stanfield is rather shy and reticent. A person of few words, he always appears to be ill at ease around people. I had the utmost respect for his intellect and sincerity, but watching him ask a question during the daily Question Period in the House of Commons was sometimes painful. He knew what he wanted to say and undoubtedly felt strongly about the subject, but he frequently appeared to have great difficulty expressing himself. This was especially true when the nature of his question demanded that he at least go through the motions of being angry.

I detected no such reticence as I watched him that morning, squatting on the sidewalk in front of Hotel Newfoundland and communicating with a tomcat. Obviously, my leader was a lover of cats. Perhaps, I thought, if I can suppress my dislike for cats long enough to give it a few strokes and a kind word or two, it will impress Stanfield and help me get back in his good books. Just as a journey of a thousand miles starts with one step, perhaps I can use the cat to help me get out of the dog house.

A survivor in Newfoundland politics for 35 years, at times I had to do things that literally made me sick, things like appeasing drunks and having to kowtow, especially at election time, to certain people who, under normal circumstances, I would walk a mile out of my way to avoid. However, there are times in the lives of most public-spirited people when they have to go the extra mile for the good of the cause. "Surely," I thought, "sharing a mutual love for cats with my party leader will do me no harm. Perhaps the next time we are together and unable to find something to talk about, we can talk about cats we have known."

It was still dark as I walked over to where Stanfield was squatting. Since I would soon be joined by Lundrigan and the other members of our party who were also booked on the early morning flight, I lost no time establishing my credentials as an avid cat lover. Obviously, Stanfield was impressed; he seemed to warm to me. He told me he always loved cats. He said that as a child he would go to his family's underwear factory in Truro to feed the cats that were kept on the premises to control the mice population.

I assured him that I too was fascinated with cats. "When I was growing up," I said, "our home was never without one." Of course, I did not tell him how we disposed of their kittens; it would not have helped my cause.

Stanfield's response to my apparent interest in the cat as it lazily stretched on the sidewalk was gratifying. However, as I began to squat down to stroke the animal, its response was anything but gratifying; it gave me a dirty look and curled its legs around Stanfield's hand, as if it wanted protection. It seemed to know what I was up to. Carefully avoiding anything that would cause the cat to turn on me, I started to run my fingers over its back, when I suddenly recognized the object on which it was bedded. I grabbed it with both hands and gave it a vicious tug, sending the cat flying through the air, screaming like blue murder. "You mangy son-of-a-bitch," I yelled. "That's my wife's skirt you're lying on." The expression on Stanfield's face is difficult to describe. He looked completely dumbfounded, unable to believe what he was seeing. He must have thought that I had suddenly gone berserk. Still squatting on the sidewalk, Stanfield looked at me as if I had just committed a mortal crime. "Why did you have to do that?" he asked. "That poor old animal was causing you no harm!"

As I knelt there, brushing the cat's hairs off my wife's skirt, I tried to explain to Stanfield what had happened. During an earlier visit to St. John's, Muriel had left one of her favourite skirts at her mother's home on Goodridge Street. She asked me to get it during my next visit to St. John's and bring it back to Ottawa with me. Returning to the hotel the previous night from a late social event, I remembered the skirt and decided to drop by and pick it up. As I was getting out of the taxi in front of the hotel, with the skirt and several other packages under my arm, I must have dropped the skirt on the sidewalk. Obviously, the cat came upon it during the night and decided to use it as a bed.

Stanfield was not amused. He slowly reverted to a standing position and walked away, shaking his head in disgust.

Ten years later, I ran into Stanfield and his wife at a Tory leadership convention in Ottawa. After we exchanged pleasantries, he shook his head and, with a deadpan expression and a look of disgust on his face, said, "Well, Carter, I still can't figure out how your wife's skirt got on the sidewalk in front of Hotel Newfoundland at five o'clock in the morning."

Thirty-two

Oops—Sorry About That!

During the nine years I spent as provincial Minister of Fisheries in the Moores, Peckford and Wells administrations, I visited every coastal community in Newfoundland and most of the communities on the Labrador Coast, using just about every means of transportation available. Since many communities were inaccessible by road, particularly those on the South Coast of Newfoundland and on the Labrador Coast, I frequently used a helicopter to get around, especially in winter when navigation was closed and heavy Arctic ice made travel even more difficult.

In February 1977 I was invited to attend the annual meeting of the Fogo Island Co-operative, which operated a major saltfish processing plant on Fogo Island. With no guarantee that the ferry service would be operating because of the presence of Arctic ice in Notre Dame Bay, I flew to Gander from St. John's and arranged to have a helicopter take me to Fogo Island. It was planned that I would attend the Co-op meeting, have lunch with the Board members and return to St. John's later in the day to attend a night sitting of the House of Assembly.

However, the meeting lasted longer than expected, and my return to St. John's had to be deferred until the following morning when the helicopter would pick me up and take me back to the city in time for the afternoon sitting of the Legislature.

As I was checking out of the motel the following morning, I ran into Aiden Maloney, who was also in Fogo attending the

Co-op meeting as Chairman of the Canadian Saltfish Corporation. I offered him a lift back to St. John's in the helicopter, which he accepted without a moment's hesitation.

The weather that morning was exceptionally pleasant. It was one of those rare mid-winter mornings with brilliant sunshine and a cloudless sky, and not a breath of wind. It was also unbearably cold. A few minutes after we boarded the helicopter and were airborne, the pilot informed us that the heating system was not working. I knew, with a cold certainty, that it wasn't going to be a pleasant trip. It was chillier in the helicopter than it was on the ground.

Unlike the helicopter pilot who was wearing a thermal jumpsuit, fur-lined boots and mitts, both Aiden and I were completely unprepared for the bone-chilling temperatures. As we flew over the Brookfield/Badger's Quay area, I was reminded of my old friend Arthur Wicks, the self-appointed, unofficial spokesman for the Bonavista North fishermen. He had achieved considerable prominence throughout the province as a regular caller to open line radio programs.

I seldom passed Badger's Quay, whether in car or helicopter, without dropping in on Arthur Wicks for a chat. An interesting and colourful character, he was not shy about voicing his opinion on almost any subject, from the price of fish to the state of the Hong Kong economy. It would be a pity, I thought, to be in the area and not drop in on Arthur and introduce him to the Chairman of the Canadian Saltfish Corporation. It would also give us a chance to thaw out over a cup of hot tea, or whatever else he chose to serve us.

The Wicks were delighted that we had dropped down for a mug-up. Never stuck for a word or a sense of humour, Arthur entertained us for an hour or so as we sat around the kitchen stove, sipping hot tea followed by a few stiff drinks of black rum.

Newfoundlanders are noted for many things, not the least of which is their preoccupation with the weather. If you meet someone on the street anywhere in Newfoundland, more often than not the greetings exchanged will be related to the weather. "Not a bad day," "Shocking weather we're having," "What's in the forecast for tomorrow?" and "Rained hard last night," are some of the most commonly used expressions. As an inshore fisherman and part-time fur trapper who spent a lifetime having to "keep an eye on the weather," Arthur was no exception. It didn't matter what we talked about, the conversation always reverted to the weather.

"Wonderful cold here last night, Walt," Arthur said. "In fact, it was so cold here last night, the old wood horse crawled up under the house for shelter." For the benefit of the uninformed, I should explain that a "wood horse" is a contraption seen in every Newfoundland outport backyard, and is used to hold in place a "turn of wood" when it is being sawed into junks for firewood.

Leaving Badger's Quay to fly over Bonavista Bay, the ocean surface was like a huge sheet of glass as far as the eye could see, completely frozen over, with not a ripple to be seen. We skirted the coastline along the southern part of Bonavista Bay, and flew over St. Brendan's, Salvage, Eastport and Musgravetown until we reached Random Island. At that point, the pilot informed us that he would have to return to Gander: the helicopter had developed a minor mechanical problem.

Rather than sit around a cold hangar in Gander while the helicopter was being checked, I instructed the pilot to drop us off in Lower Lance Cove, on the eastern end of Random Island. Aiden and I could visit my wife's brother Allan Baker and his wife Iris, who had just taken over her family's general store there. We desperately needed some place to thaw out and get another cup of hot tea.

Iris' parents, Arch and Doris Ivany, were typical outport business people. Their lives were completely wrapped up in their home and general store, both of which were meticulously cared for and kept spotlessly clean.

The Ivany home was a large old-fashioned, two-story structure, with grates in the living and dining rooms, and a large wood-and-coal stove in the kitchen, which was only used in case of a power failure or other emergency. They also had an electric stove in the kitchen, on which they baked and cooked.

In every nook and cranny, including the kitchen, there was evidence that someone had spent many hours sitting in the old-fashioned rocking chair knitting clothing, crocheting cloths and sewing patchwork quilts. It still occupied a prominent place in the kitchen, complemented by beautiful hand-crocheted doilies and embroidered cloths on almost every flat surface. Decorative, multi-coloured quilts, handmade bedspreads and pillow cases adorned the beds in each bedroom. The Ivany home, and most of its contents, represented countless hours of hard work and patience on the part of its owners.

It was also a home that did not lack warmth and hospitality. Almost before we got a chance to take off our coats, Aiden and I were being treated to a delicious meal, preceded by a cup of hot tea that we needed badly. We were still feeling the effects of the hour we had spent sitting in a helicopter without heat.

As we enjoyed the warm hospitality of our hosts, the time passed too quickly, and before we knew it the helicopter was circling overhead as it prepared to take us on the final leg of our journey to St. John's.

For some inexplicable reason, most people, especially those who live in the more isolated communities, are fascinated with helicopters. They cannot seem to resist the urge to stand around and watch them land and take off. The Ivanys were no different. When we were ready to leave, Iris and her mother, bundled up in heavy parkas, stood in the front garden to watch the helicopter leave the ground. Arch Ivany, who was suffering with a cold, decided to watch from the kitchen window.

The helicopter hovered about fifty feet over the Ivany house while we waved and shouted our good-byes. Wind from its blade was having a tornado effect on the snow on the ground, causing it to swirl in all directions. Suddenly, Arch Ivany came running from the house, frantically waving his arms as he struggled to brace himself against the wind and the snow being stirred up by the helicopter. He hurried toward the spot where Iris and her mother were standing, shouting and pointing towards the house. Losing all interest in the helicopter, they suddenly ran as fast as they could towards the house, scrambling through the front door.

Even though I was curious to know why the Ivanys had acted so strangely, it was not until I arrived home that I found out what had happened. As I entered the driveway, my wife Muriel was in the doorway waiting for me. She was devastated. "How are we ever going to face the Ivanys again?" she kept saying. "You have ruined their home and everything in it." Caught completely by surprise, I asked Muriel to start from the beginning and tell me what had happened. Surely, I thought, my brief visit to the Ivany home didn't cause it and its contents to be ruined.

It seems that as we were hovering above the Ivany home in the helicopter, wind from its blades not only caused the snow to violently swirl around the front garden, it also caused a backdraft in the two chimneys, spewing their contents throughout the house. Soot that had accumulated for years came belching out of the fireplaces in the living and dining rooms and through the grating in the kitchen stove. Everything in the house, including its owner, was covered with soot.

In his desperation to close the damper and prevent the soot from going all over the house, Arch Ivany suddenly took on the appearance of a vaudeville minstrel. He was covered

from head to foot with soot. Later, as Iris described the incident and the shock they experienced upon entering the house, she said her father "was as black as the ace of spades." Temporarily blinded by the bright sunshine outside, "as we entered the house, all I could see were the whites of his eyes."

Being the kind of people they were, the Ivanys took things in stride and immediately started the process of cleaning up the mess. I was truly sorry for what had happened and offered to accept responsibility for the cost of having professional cleaners do a complete housecleaning job. But the Ivanys would not hear of it. "It couldn't be helped," they said. "It's nothing that a good scrubbing won't remedy."

Several months passed before I had the occasion and the courage to revisit the Ivanys. I felt somewhat sheepish at first, remembering the helicopter incident and the resultant chaos that our impromptu farewell had caused. However, I soon discovered that not only was there no trace of the soot to be seen anywhere in their home, there was not a trace of rancour or ill feeling towards me for what had happened.

Even Arch Ivany, restored to his original colour, bore me no animosity. Such is the forgiveness of friends.

INDEX